MW01675486

SHOWING SOCIAL SOLIDARITY WITH FUTURE GENERATIONS

Today's generations can affect the future ecosystem more than any previous generations and aggravate the welfare of future people. Children and people who have not yet been born are excluded from political decisions important to their lives. Due to the future generations' lack of influence, current generations have a responsibility to act.

The current generation's responsibility for the well-being of future generations has been used as an argument for an increasing number of legislative and policy measures across the world but are rarely followed up in practice.

This book examines when commitments to future generations are followed up in practice and in what situations they are not.

A concept of solidarity with future generations is developed and applied to four policy areas: the UN 2030 Agenda, national political institutions for future generations, constitutions and climate lawsuits, and regulations of economic debt or savings for future generations. Germany and Norway are selected as cases to evaluate what the commitments might entail in practice.

The book highlights where the gaps emerge, and what needs to be done. The failing transition from the global to the national level highlights a need for stronger cosmopolitan elements in the international political system. Institutional bindings are generally weak at the national level. Financial restrictions show that it is possible to establish strong institutional constraints, but the focus on financial resources is too narrow. Both national and global institutional bindings must be strengthened to show social solidarity with future generations.

Marianne Takle is a research professor at Norwegian Social Research at Oslo Metropolitan University, Norway. She has been a visiting fellow at POLIS, University of Cambridge and Europa-Kollege, Universität Hamburg. She has co-edited two books newly published by Routledge: Falch-Eriksen, A., Takle, M., and Slagsvold, B. (Eds.) (2021), *Generational Tensions and Solidarity Within Advanced Welfare States*; and Takle et al. (Eds.) (2023), *Citizenship and Social Exclusion at the Margins of the Welfare State.*

Routledge Advances in Health and Social Policy

Inciting Justice and Progressive Power
The Partnership for Working Families Cities
Edited by David Reynolds and Louise Simmons

Death, Grief and Loss in the Context of COVID-19
Edited by Panagiotis Pentaris

Charity and Poverty in Advanced Welfare States
Cameron Parsell, Andrew Clarke and Francisco Perales

Child and Youth Participation in Policy, Practice and Research
Edited by Deirdre Horgan and Danielle Kennan

Social Suffering in the Neoliberal Age
Edited by Karen Soldatic and Louise St Guillaume

Responding to Domestic Violence
Difficult Conversations
Kate Seymour, Sarah Wendt and Kristin Natalier

Showing Social Solidarity with Future Generations
Marianne Takle

For more information about this series, please visit: https://www.routledge.com/Routledge-Advances-in-Health-and-Social-Policy/book-series/RAHSP

SHOWING SOCIAL SOLIDARITY WITH FUTURE GENERATIONS

Marianne Takle

Routledge
Taylor & Francis Grou
LONDON AND NEW YOR

Designed cover image: Photo by Håvard Takle Lindholm

First published 2025
by Routledge
4 Park Square, Milton Park, Abingdon, Oxon OX14 4RN

and by Routledge
605 Third Avenue, New York, NY 10158

Routledge is an imprint of the Taylor & Francis Group, an informa business

© 2025 **Marianne Takle**

The right of **Marianne Takle** to be identified as author of this work has been asserted in accordance with sections 77 and 78 of the Copyright, Designs and Patents Act 1988.

The Open Access version of this book, available at www.taylorfrancis.com, has been made available under a Creative Commons Attribution-Non Commercial-No Derivatives (CC-BY-NC-ND) 4.0 license.

Any third party material in this book is not included in the OA Creative Commons license, unless indicated otherwise in a credit line to the material. Please direct any permissions enquiries to the original rightsholder.

Trademark notice: Product or corporate names may be trademarks or registered trademarks, and are used only for identification and explanation without intent to infringe.

British Library Cataloguing-in-Publication Data
A catalogue record for this book is available from the British Library

Library of Congress Cataloging-in-Publication Data
Names: Takle, Marianne, author.
Title: Showing social solidarity with future generations / Marianne Takle.
Description: Abingdon, Oxon ; New York, NY : Routledge, 2025. | Series: Routledge advances in health and social policy | Includes bibliographical references and index. | Contents: Part I. Solidarity in Theory -- What is solidarity? -- Temporality, narratives, and generations -- Solidarity with future generations -- Part II. Solidarity in Practice -- The UN 2030 Agenda and future generations -- National political institutions for future generations -- Constitutions, protection clauses and climate lawsuits -- Economic debt and savings for future generations. | Identifiers: LCCN 2024028695 (print) | LCCN 2024028696 (ebook) | ISBN 9781032510330 (hardback) | ISBN 9781032510385 (paperback) | ISBN 9781003400806 (ebook)
Subjects: LCSH: Sustainable development. | Intergenerational relations--Social aspects. | Intergenerational relations--Economic aspects. | Environmental management. | Solidarity. | Future, The.
Classification: LCC HC79.E5 T35248 2025 (print) | LCC HC79.E5 (ebook) | DDC 338.9/27--dc23/eng/20240715
LC record available at https://lccn.loc.gov/2024028695
LC ebook record available at https://lccn.loc.gov/2024028696

ISBN: 978-1-032-51033-0 (hbk)
ISBN: 978-1-032-51038-5 (pbk)
ISBN: 978-1-003-40080-6 (ebk)

DOI: 10.4324/9781003400806

Typeset in Sabon
by KnowledgeWorks Global Ltd.

CONTENTS

ACKNOWLEDGEMENTS

This book was written within the framework of the project Sustainable Societies in the 21st Century: From Welfare States to Eco-social States. I thank NOVA, Oslo Metropolitan University, for its financial support. I also thank my colleagues at the Section for Health and Welfare Studies at NOVA for their valuable comments on the project. I especially thank the head of the section, Janikke Solstad Vedeler, for her encouragement and for making my working life easier. I am very grateful that Kristian Heggebø used his sharp eyes to read the whole book and gave me valuable comments. I am glad that Mi Ah Schoyen read essential parts of the book and gave useful input, as so many times before. I am grateful to Asgeir Falch-Eriksen because one of his brilliant ideas saved the project when I did not understand how to finish it. I am thankful that Terry Lane has excellently edited the language, as he has done so many times for more than a decade.

The research group Media, Environment, and Society at Oslo Metropolitan University has been an important source of inspiration. I am grateful that the members commented on different versions of the book. I am especially thankful that the group leader, Andreas Ytterstad, gave me constructive comments. I would like to thank Jörg Tremmel and Steffen Suur-Nuuja for their valuable comments on the part of the book dealing with German politics.

I am grateful that Dagny Stuedahl invited me to present the manuscript at the Henrik Steffens-Masterclass series – Nature, Thinking, Acting – at the Humboldt University of Berlin. The discussions with the young people attending the course inspired me to think even more about the responsibilities today's adult generation has towards those who come after us. An important thank you goes to the youths who frequent our home: Håvard Takle Lindholm, Kath Heck, Østein Takle Lindholm, and Ingebjørg Arneberg

Stueland. Our discussions have been an essential inspiration. I also owe Øystein Takle Lindholm thanks for excellent comments on parts of the book. I am grateful to my 90-year-old mother for her daily encouragement to complete the project.

Most of all, I am grateful for all the support I have received from my husband, Magne Lindholm. He has read and commented on countless versions of the manuscript, and thanks to our discussions, it finally became a book. Any errors that may have occurred in the book are of course my own responsibility.

ABBREVIATIONS

ECHR	European Convention on Human Rights
ECtHR	European Court of Human Rights
EU	European Union
GDP	Gross Domestic Product
HLPF	High-level Political Forum on Sustainable Development
IEA	International Energy Agency
IMF	International Monetary Fund
IPBES	Intergovernmental Platform on Biodiversity and Ecosystem Services
IPCC	Intergovernmental Panel on Climate Change
MDGs	Millennium Development Goals
NBIM	Norges Bank Investment Management
NIM	Norwegian Human Rights Institution
OECD	Organisation for Economic Co-operation and Development
PBnE	German Parliamentary Advisory Council on Sustainable Development
PDO	Plan for Development and Operation
RNE	German Council for Sustainable Development
SDGs	Sustainable Development Goals
SRU	German Advisory Council on the Environment
UN	United Nations
UNEP	United Nations Environment Programme
UNESCO	United Nations Educational, Scientific and Cultural Organization
WBGU	German Advisory Council on Global Change
WCED	World Commission on Environment and Development

1 INTRODUCTION

Challenges for future generations

Today's generations can affect the future ecosystem more than any previous generations and thereby significantly influence the welfare of future people. A study published in *Science* in 2021 shows this clearly: Thiery and his colleagues compared people aged above 55 years with six-year-old children in 2020. Under a "current policies" scenario, which is estimated to limit global warming to below 3°C by 2100, they project that a six-year-old child will experience: "Twice as many wildfires and tropical cyclones, three times more river floods, four times more crop failures, five times more droughts, and 36 times more heat waves relative to the reference person" (Thiery et al., 2021, pp. 158–159).

The authors note that limiting the warming to 1.5°C reduces the burdens, but it still leaves the younger generations with far more significant burdens than the older generations. The Intergovernmental Panel on Climate Change (IPCC) Sixth Assessment Report from 2023 has similar future projections of differences in climate exposure for generations born in 1950, 1980, and 2020 (IPCC, 2023). These well-documented and widely supported projections highlight a severe threat to the safety of younger generations compared to the older generations.

While current generations influence future generations' welfare, people who have not yet been born are excluded from contemporary political decisions which will be important for their lives. As the UN World Commission on Environment and Development emphasised nearly 40 years ago, "we act as we do because we can get away with it: future generations do not vote; they have no political or financial power; they cannot challenge our

DOI: 10.4324/9781003400806-1
This chapter has been made available under a CC-BY-NC-ND 4.0 license.

decisions" (WCED, 1987, Chapter 1, No. 25). Due to this combination of current generations' capacity to affect future generations' welfare more than ever and future generations' lack of influence, political and academic debates have arisen about the current generations' responsibility.

According to the UN Secretary-General, at least 394 General Assembly Resolutions explicitly mentioned "future generations" between 1961 and 2023 (UN Policy Brief, 2023). In addition, commitments to future generations are included in UN declarations, Secretary-General reports, and policy briefs, and they cut across all issue areas. All these documents show that the norm that today's generations should take their descendants into account is well established in the UN. This norm is also evident within several nation states, where increasingly more political and legal measures are justified with reference to a concern for future generations (Dirth & Kormann da Silva, 2022; Linehan & Lawrence, 2021; Segger et al., 2021).

However, it is also well documented that these commitments are rarely followed up in practice. Several analyses show that too little is implemented, too slowly, and too late (Thunberg, 2022). One example is the findings from the 2023 edition of the Production Gap Report (UNEP, 2023). It reveals that the 20 major fossil-fuel-producing countries in the world plan to produce around 110% more fossil fuels in 2030 than would be consistent with limiting warming to 1.5°C, leading to a production gap. The report shows that the countries' combined plans will increase global coal production until 2030 and global oil and gas production until at least 2050, creating an ever-widening production gap for fossil fuels over time (UNEP, 2023).

This well-known discrepancy between commitments to the future and a lack of follow-up has led to moral indignation and questions about why the commitments do not lead to actions. In this book, I analyse political and legal measures where we can find explicitly formulated normative commitments to take into account the concerns of future generations in current political decisions. The analysis concentrates on four empirical examples:

- The UN 2030 Agenda with the 17 Sustainable Development Goals (SDGs)
- National political institutions for future generations
- National constitutions with protection clauses for future generations
- Regulations of national economic debt or savings for future generations

While the first is at the global level, the remaining three are at the national level. In these examples, concerns for future generations are expressed both globally and nationally, and they show commitments that encompass political, legal, and economic policy issues. The empirical studies are from Germany and Norway as both are examples of countries that have referred to a concern for future generations in these policy areas. These country cases allow us to evaluate what such concerns might entail.

The overarching questions analysed in this book concern when and how the commitments to future generations are followed up in practice, and what characterises situations where they are not followed up. To what extent and how are there differences between Germany and Norway within the four policy areas outlined earlier, and what can we learn from comparing them?

To analyse these questions, I have developed a concept of solidarity with future generations, which can be operationalised and applied to empirical analyses. What it might mean to act in solidarity with future people has been discussed previously in few theoretical and philosophical studies. They have developed normative concepts and principles that are challenging to apply to empirical studies (Bazzani, 2023; Gómez-Franco, 2024; Tong et al., 2023).

It is still unclear what the concept of solidarity with the people of the future entails and how such a concept can be applied to empirical studies of practical politics. Therefore, this book starts by defining what solidarity among contemporaries means and elaborates on how this concept can be extended to include young people and people who will be born in the future. The aim is to establish a theoretically grounded concept of solidarity with future generations that can be applied in empirical studies. To do this, I draw on insights from a wide range of studies about future generations including political philosophy, political science, law studies, and welfare economics, and combine these with a normative-political concept of solidarity. The intention is to improve our understanding of the normative basis for including a concern for future generations in current political processes and apply this to empirical studies.

This chapter first clarifies what is meant by future generations in this book. The second section describes the policy areas where political and legal measures are justified by referring to future generations. The third section discusses how future generations are often studied from the perspective of intergenerational justice and how a concept of solidarity can contribute to new understandings. The fourth section defines solidarity among contemporaries, and the fifth elaborates on how solidarity can be extended to include future generations. The sixth section discusses democratic myopia, and the seventh explains why Germany and Norway are selected as examples. The eighth section presents the methodology and the structure of the book.

Who are the future generations?

When discussing future generations, we often refer to our children and grandchildren, perhaps also great-grandchildren. They are people we have met or can easily imagine. People of different ages living together at any given time are called overlapping generations.

Future generations can also be understood as people who have not yet been born. They are likely to be born but there is uncertainty regarding exactly who, where, and when. They are people we know little or nothing about, beyond the fact that they will live in a world we leave behind. In contrast to currently living young people, unborn future generations cannot raise their voice. This implies current generations' understandings and decisions are decisive for future generations' welfare.

These two ways of defining future generations overlap and are often used interchangeably. In this book, the concept of future generations refers to children and young people living today as well as unborn generations. It neither defines children and young people based on a specific age limit nor the number of future unborn generations to include in the analysis. The intention is to analyse the extent to which and how contemporary political decisions include children and young people with weak political influence as well as people who have not yet been born and have no influence. The term intergenerational relations is also used to describe this relationship, as opposed to intragenerational relations, a topic which focuses on relations within generations (Tremmel, 2009).

Moreover, in the scholarly literature various concerns regarding future generations are expressed in terms of future generations' needs, capabilities, welfare, well-being, health, interests, resources, representation, or rights. These expressions overlap in practice as they are all concerned with whether future people should be given the opportunity to live dignified lives. What current generations should ensure so that future generations get these different opportunities depends on the context. This book mainly concentrates on discussions about giving future generations representation, rights, and resources. The expression of concern for future generations is used as a general reference to the inclusion of young and unborn people in contemporary political and legal considerations. Many of the fundamental questions discussed concern people who have not yet been born.

Commitments to future generations

An approach to future generations commonly used in political and academic debates was set in 1987 by how the UN World Commission on Environment and Development defined sustainable development as "Sustainable development is development that meets the needs of the present without compromising the ability of future generations to meet their own needs" (WCED, 1987, Chapter 2, No. 1). Sustainable development is connected to long-term thinking and commitments to future generations. Accordingly, commitments to future generations can be regulated by providing future generations' rights, representation, and resources. The empirical analyses are based on comparative studies of Germany and Norway, and the reasons for selecting these countries are outlined below. The following four paragraphs present the examples studied in each of the empirical chapters of this book, i.e. Chapters 5–8.

Firstly, commitment to future generations is at the heart of the UN declaration *Transforming our World: The 2030 Agenda for Sustainable Development* (UN 2030 Agenda, 2015). This was adopted by 193 UN member states in 2015. These commitments are integral to the agenda's 17 SDGs and 169 associated targets. By encouraging national governments to fulfil the goals and targets, the 2030 Agenda can contribute to the implementation of commitments to future generations. This presupposes that the SDGs are met, which depends on how the individual nation states translate these goals into practical actions (Segger et al., 2021).

Secondly, there are many types of national institutions that take future generations into account. While these can be categorised in different ways, this book distinguishes between two types. One type is established to implement the 2030 Agenda with the SDGs. This type of institution does not particularly focus on future generations but offers a broad institutional framework for long-term policy. The other type is designed to have a specific mission for future generations. According to Dirth and Kormann da Silva (2022), 16 countries in the world have established this second type of institutions. These mainly take the form of committees established within parliamentary systems and government bodies, or as independent institutions to represent future generations (Brown Weiss, 2021; Tremmel, 2021). Based on their design and tasks, these two types of institution can be distinct, but in practice, they overlap in that both aim to secure a long-term policy. By establishing such institutions, countries have committed themselves to taking future people's concerns into account in current policy, and some of them give future generations proxy representation.

Thirdly, national constitutions are a modern states' most important intergenerational contracts. They are intended to endure for many generations and can thus be seen as self-imposed political and legal bindings for current generations (Gosseries, 2014). Studies show that 30 countries in the world have formulated protection clauses for future generations referring to the environment and sustainability in their constitutions (Dirth, 2018; Tremmel, 2006). However, the practical consequences of protection clauses depend on whether they are followed up in practice. These clauses have created a new arena for both adults and young people defending the rights of future generations. Setzer and Higham (2022; 2023) registered 2,341 climate litigations worldwide between 1986 and 2023. Their success or failure can reveal whether future generations achieve rights through self-imposed constraints on today's generations.

Fourthly, many countries have high public debts. This means that future generations will pay for the current generations' spendings. Over the past two decades, a growing number of countries worldwide have adopted fiscal rules, which are long-standing limitations on public budgets. By 2021, 105 countries had adopted at least one budget rule (Davoodi et al., 2022).

Advanced countries, particularly in Europe, are frontrunners in this trend. Budget restrictions are often justified with references to self-imposed bindings for the sake of future generations. These economic constraints raise questions regarding the kind of resources that are transferred between generations.

Intergenerational justice and solidarity

The responsibility of today's generations for future generations is often studied from the perspective of intergenerational justice. Theories of intergenerational justice consider if and how justice can be applied in relations between generations with the focus on the uncertainty about the lives of unborn persons, and the lack of reciprocity between generations. The various theories offer different normative solutions to these problems, and they thus point in different directions (Gosseries & Meyer, 2011).

Within a liberal political tradition, two approaches are particularly useful for discussing how one generation determines the nature of its responsibilities for future generations. One is Rawls' (1971, 2001) proposal for justice as impartiality, while the other is Gosseries' (2011) theories of intergenerational reciprocity. Both are contractual approaches to intergenerational justice founded on theories of justice between contemporaries and adapted to justice between current and future generations. They are chosen because they offer judgements about principles of intergenerational justice. Rawls' contribution was one of the earliest in the debate on intergenerational justice and has influenced subsequent debate on the topic. Gosseries' contribution offers useful discussions on how reciprocity can be redefined as indirect reciprocity. While Gosseries does not discuss solidarity, reciprocity is, as discussed in the next section, a core dimension of the concept of solidarity with future generations.

These theories provide us with abstract principles of justice that can be applied in different contexts that extend globally and include future generations. Studies of intergenerational justice are thus a good starting point for analysing the concern for future generations as they generally capture the uncertainties, complexities, and tensions underlying these concerns (Lawrence, 2014; Tremmel, 2009). They are, however, insufficient to analyse collective commitments to the future and how they are implemented in practice, which is central to the consideration of future generations.

We need more practical analytical tools that can be applied in empirical analyses. Accordingly, this book develops a concept of solidarity with future generations as the main analytical tool and applies it to the four policy examples mentioned earlier. Justice is a part of the concept of solidarity, but solidarity is more comprehensive. Like some approaches to justice, solidarity assumes equality and reciprocity between people, but it is more binding (Habermas, 2015). Solidarity encompasses social norms and practices that are ensured and maintained through legal and political institutions (Banting & Kymlicka, 2017).

This combination of social norms with political and institutional bindings defines social solidarity in this book. Appeals to showing social solidarity are calls for action to correct injustice. With this book, I aim to contribute to political and academic debates by combining the scholarly literature on future generations with that on solidarity.

Solidarity

Solidarity is a central concept in political thinking, but there is no standard definition. The interpretation fluctuates depending on the context in which the concept is used and the understanding of the involved actors (Stjernø, 2005). This book's understanding of solidarity builds on theories that emphasise how solidarity among contemporaries is based on shared commitments of a community, which goes beyond both self-interests and rights-based humanitarian obligations (Banting & Kymlicka, 2017; Habermas, 2015; Stjernø, 2005). Solidarity requires more of the individual actors than a pooling of interests and involves more than justice. It requires a form of political community based on expectations of reciprocity.

I define solidarity by making a distinction between two dimensions that, in combination, constitute the concept. The first dimension of solidarity is reciprocity and mutual obligations among equal individuals with shared values, goals, or interests (Stjernø, 2005). This concerns ideas, attitudes, and motivation. In simple terms this means that "one day you need help, another day I need help." As we do not know when each of us will need help, we support each other in solidarity. The second dimension of solidarity is people's willingness to enter collective binding constraints through institutions (Banting & Kymlicka, 2017). This is the implementation of commitments in practice – in the form of institutional bindings. These bindings can be amendments of existing institutions or the establishment of new institutions. Institutions are defined as a combination of a meaning structure that explains and justifies the rules of conduct and a resource structure that makes it possible to act according to the rules (March & Olsen, 1995).

Moreover, I study macro-level solidarity, mainly at the nation state level, where people do not meet face to face but still imagine a sense of community that solidarity requires (Anderson, 1991). National solidarity encompasses all members of a political community within the borders of nation states. At the national level, there are legal and political institutions ensuring that the ideas and motivations for commitments are realised in practice. Today's cross-border challenges create a need to discuss how solidarity can be extended to cover the world. This would be a cosmopolitan solidarity involving notions of a community encompassing all people around the globe (Jakobsen, 2009).

There are no global institutions which correspond to the national institutions, but there are institutions such as the UN, the International Court of Justice, and the European Court of Human Rights.

Solidarity with future generations

My aim is to elaborate on theoretically grounded normative arguments about how this two-dimensional concept of solidarity can be extended to include people who will be born in the future. This means the inclusion of people who have not yet been born and therefore cannot give anything back, and there is no equality between generations.

To the first dimension of solidarity, reciprocity fails to provide adequate justification for our obligations towards future generations. This is thus redefined as indirect reciprocity. This means giving something to a person, but it is not necessarily the same person who gives you something in return (Gosseries, 2011; Tremmel, 2021). In simple terms, it can be formulated as "I help you, and someone else within our political community helps me." Indirect reciprocity can take the form of the current generation transferring something of value to its succeeding generation, which the current generation itself has received from previous generations.

The second dimension of solidarity is the current generations' willingness to establish self-imposed institutional bindings with long-term goals. Such bindings are ways of following up the commitments to take future generations' concerns into account. The bindings put institutional constraints on political actors to follow an agreed course of action or agreed norms or rules (Boston, 2021). Legal and political institutions can help to reduce long-term compliance problems by increasing the costs of taking the easy way out. This dimension differs from solidarity with contemporaries in that the time perspective on the bindings is central. The purpose is to bind political actors to follow long-term goals by making it problematic to break with the goals without high costs.

The two dimensions must be combined in order to show social solidarity with future generations. To say something more substantial about what forms the relations between them in various policy areas, new empirical analyses are conducted in Chapters 5–8.

Democratic myopia

Crucial for understanding the challenges to long-term policies is the extent to which contemporary understandings of time and political institutions are designed for solving current problems. The interests of future generations often fall short when there are tensions between the interests of current and future generations (Caney, 2018; Jones et al., 2018). In democracies, this is described as "democratic myopia," which is the tendency of short-sightedness in both mindset and institutional structures of democratic decision-making processes (MacKenzie, 2021; Smith, 2021). The mindset involves framing, which means choosing some information over others and making them more salient to promote a particular problem definition, moral evaluation, and recommendations (Entman, 1993).

Democratic myopia can be understood through at least three key political dynamics involving combinations of short-sighted mindsets or frames and institutional structures. One is that the electoral terms in most democracies are between four and six years. This leads to politicians focusing on the next election and preferring short-term decisions at the cost of long-term strategies. To this dynamic, we can add that the electoral calculations of politicians often rest on the belief that the voters are short-sighted (Tremmel, 2015), and studies show that only a minority of individuals support policies for future generations (Busemeyer, 2024).

Another political dynamic is that government departments often work in silos and are problematic to coordinate (Schoyen & Takle, 2022). Solving long-term problems, such as environmental destruction, requires cooperation and holistic thinking. This proves challenging to achieve also because politicians are responsive to interest groups and powerful lobby groups (Smith, 2021).

A third political dynamic is that democratic institutions are deeply constrained and conditioned by global capitalism (Smith, 2021). Governments often leave decisions to the market, and this is problematic in terms of future challenges because market logic is based on short-term thinking (MacKenzie, 2021). There is a tendency to discount the future in favour of today. This means that measures for progress and return on investment are higher in the short term and are therefore more important than what is expected to come in the longer term (Maxton & Randers, 2016). Moreover, the "growth paradigm" dominates current economic thinking, and this structural incentive makes it challenging to follow long-term social and environmental goals within a capitalist economy (Büchs & Koch, 2017; Koch, 2023). Finally, economic results are used as an indicator of progress in national income accounting. The production of goods and services is based on growth and monetary values, while the importance of nature is often sidelined (Pascual et al., 2023).

These political dynamics form a backdrop for understanding what shapes the relationship between current generations' commitments to future generations and the establishment of politically and legally binding institutions.

MacAskill (2022) has called for long-termism in the sense that future people count, and that today's generations can influence their lives. The point that today's generations can affect the people of the future is obvious, but what to do about it is more controversial. MacAskill's (2022) "what to do list" is only based on what single individuals can do. This book concentrates on commitments to binding collective solutions.

Why Germany and Norway?

There are significant social and economic inequalities in the world. These differences are closely linked to historical circumstances which have created the differences between the global North and South, contemporary production systems, and carbon emissions. The richest 1% of the world's population in the global North is responsible for more than twice as much carbon pollution as the people who make up the poorest 50% in the global South (Thunberg, 2022). Those who suffer most from environmental destruction are rarely those who caused it. Moreover, the projected threat to the safety of younger generations compared to older generations highlights a particular increase in lifetime exposure to extreme events in the Middle East and North Africa (Thiery et al., 2021, pp. 158–159).

There is a need for many forms of knowledge in a world with environmental challenges where there are major differences between those responsible for the destruction and those who suffer the most. Climate change and biodiversity science are needed. Furthermore, we need knowledge about the countries of the global North with a special responsibility to reduce greenhouse gas emissions and ensure biological diversity, as was established in the principle of "common but differentiated responsibilities" (UN Earth Summit in Rio de Janeiro, 1992). This responsibility is an important motivation for carrying out empirical studies in Europe.

I have selected Germany and Norway as cases and conduct a comparative study. These two countries have been selected because both have apparent dilemmas linked to ecological, political, and economic development that require both immediate solutions and long-term thinking. Moreover, Germany and Norway are similar with respect to several topics discussed in this book. Both countries are at the forefront of implementing the UN's SDGs, they have a constitutional ecological posterity clause, and self-imposed national budget restrictions. These two countries are highly developed welfare states and democracies in which public justification and contestation of legislative and policy measures are required and expected. At the same time, they differ in the political contexts in which the legislative and policy measures are justified, contested, and implemented.

The German case represents a vital dilemma between the urgent need to consider secure alternative energy supplies because of the Russian invasion of Ukraine in February 2022, and the need for long-term thinking to safeguard the welfare of future generations. While the German Renewable Energy Law from 2000 was a step in the transition from fossil fuels to renewable energy, the *Energiewende* became a key in German climate and environmental policy after the Fukushima nuclear disaster in 2011. All major political parties agreed to phase out Germany's nuclear power plants by 2022, and this required an acceleration in the transition to renewable energy. Internationally, the *Energiewende* has been celebrated as an image of global leadership in climate policy (Schoyen et al., 2022).

However, Russia's invasion of Ukraine revealed that this policy rested on unstable political premises. Gas from Russia was seen as a pure bridge technology, compared to nuclear power and coal, until the transition to renewable energy sources was completed. Russia was Germany's leading energy supplier. In 2021, Russia accounted for 55% of Germany's gas imports (Statista, 2023). With the Russian invasion of Ukraine, a new geopolitical aspect entered the debate, in which security, freedom, and sovereignty are decisive for political considerations (Wiertz et al., 2023). The *Energiewende* is no longer only about trade-offs between energy supply, climate change, and economic and social conditions.

In the German case, the security aspects of the transition to renewable energy come to the fore. In simple terms, the dilemma consists of the fact that if Germany takes security policy considerations into account, it will involve expensive energy and increased consumption of fossil fuels, at least in the short term. This has led to more significant disagreements about the future direction in how to balance energy supply, economy, and security. Today's government is trying both to find alternative energy sources, which also involve fossil fuels such as liquefied natural gas, and to simultaneously accelerate the transition to renewable energy.

The Norwegian case represents an interesting paradox. Internationally, Norway aims to take the lead in solving climate and environmental challenges. At the same time, the country is an important contributor to these challenges through its petroleum activities. Norway is the third largest gas exporter in the world and the 15th largest oil exporter (Norwegian Petroleum, 2023). This production, and the infrastructure supporting it, are of considerable importance to the Norwegian state's income. As summarised in a report to the UN Human Rights Council in March 2020,

> the Norwegian paradox is that its leadership in addressing the global climate emergency is undermined in some areas by its ongoing dependence on a large petroleum industry. Norway is one of the world's largest exporters of oil and natural gas. The combined value of oil and gas represents almost half of the total value of national exports. Emissions from this sector have increased substantially since 1992 and exploration for additional oil and gas continues, despite clear evidence that if existing reserves of oil, gas and coal are burned, the targets established in the Paris Agreement cannot be met.
>
> *(UN General Assembly, 2020, p. 8)*

In the Norwegian case, the challenges to the welfare state come to the fore. The country's most important industry, petroleum activities, is set against one of the most important environmental challenges the world is facing: climate change. Within the context of a welfare state economically dependent on income from its large petroleum industry, the Norwegian case throws light on how long-term concern for protecting the environment – also for those who come after us – conflicts with the challenges it poses to today's welfare state.

Germany and Norway are interesting examples for studying if and how future concerns are integrated into contemporary political decisions. The German dilemma is that the transition to renewable energy is based on an uncertain energy supply, where security policy aspects are central. The Norwegian paradox is based on a double standard, where one favours global climate and environmental policy and the other means it is an important contributor to fossil fuel extraction and export. Moreover, both countries' decisions in the short and long term will have an impact on other countries. Germany's size and position in the middle of Europe gives the country influence, particularly within the European Union (EU). Although Norway is small, it has the world's largest sovereign wealth fund, and it is a large exporter of gas and oil. With its investments in around 9,000 companies worldwide, the fund is the largest single owner in the world's stock markets, owning almost 1.5% of all shares in the world's listed companies (NBIM, 2024). Norway's oil production covers about 2% of the global demand, and its natural gas production covers approximately 3%. Norway supplies between 20% and 25% of the EU's and United Kingdom's gas demand (Norwegian Petroleum, 2024).

Germany is a full member of the EU and is integrated into the European Monetary Union with the euro as the common currency. This entails stricter legal, political, and economic frameworks for German politics. While Norway is not a member of the EU, the country is integrated in many policy areas through the European Economic Area (EEA) agreement.

Methodology and structure of the book

This book is written as a monograph. The individual chapters are linked and form a whole, although each chapter has a list of references. The research design involves comparing two countries and four different policy areas: the implementation of the UN's 2030 Agenda, political institutions for future generations, constitutions with a protection clause for future generations, and budget rules that are based on the consideration of future generations. Except for the analysis of the 2030 Agenda, the purpose of these comparisons between and within the countries is to analyse the specific challenges these countries face and to find the differences between the policy areas. Furthermore, based on these empirical analyses, some tentatively general conclusions are drawn (Andersen, 2013). The overall aim is to enhance our understanding of how current political and legal measures respond to challenges with an increased need for long-term solutions. The intention is not to predict what will happen in the future. The book addresses today's solutions, or lack thereof, to take account of those who come after us.

The study is based on document analysis. It uses a practice-oriented method that discusses arguments and discourses used in the documents and the political processes and institutions they are a part of (Asdahl & Reinertsen, 2021). The documents are studied as a form of practice and what the various actors do with the documents. This involves an assessment of the documents concerning their function in the different political processes, such as who writes them, who are the sender and recipient, and what actions the documents lead to.

The empirical studies are carried out in the four different policy areas and are based on various types of documents. The introductions to each of the empirical studies, in Chapters 5–8, present the specific documents that inform the analysis in that chapter. Common to all empirical studies is that the investigations into indirect reciprocity, the first dimension of solidarity with future generations, are based on analyses of commitments expressed in laws, political agreements, and declarations. To analyse the extent to which commitments towards future generations are followed up in practice, the second dimension of solidarity is investigated, whether and how self-imposed constraints entail institutional amendments or the establishment of new institutions. While most documents are official translations into English published by the participating actors studied, some documents are unofficial translations. In cases where I have translated from German or Norwegian into English, this is noted in the reference.

The analysis concentrates on commitments and institutions for future generations and does not include explicit justifications related to animals or nature itself. These types of considerations are closely connected (Lawrence, 2022). Humans depend on a well-functioning planet to live, and this also includes animals.

The book builds on and further develops my previous work on the topic. The analysis of UN Agenda 2030 and future generations is based on an article published in *International Relations* in 2021 (Takle, 2021a). The study of German and Norwegian institutionalisation of the implementation of the UN 2030 Agenda with the SDGs builds on two chapters co-authored with colleagues and published in *Towards Sustainable Welfare States in Europe, Social Policy and Climate Change* in 2022 (Schoyen & Takle, 2022; Schoyen et al., 2022). The study of constitution, protection clauses, and lawsuits in Norway further develops two chapters published in the edited books *Generational Tensions and Solidarity Within Advanced Welfare States* in 2021 (Takle, 2021b) and *Citizenship and Social Exclusion at the Margins of the Welfare State* in 2023 (Takle, 2023). The analysis of Norwegian savings for future generations further develops an article in *Environmental Values* in 2021 (Takle, 2021c).

This book is divided into two parts. The first part, Chapters 2–4, defines the main theoretical concept used in the book. Chapter 2 discusses how the concept of solidarity is understood in central academic contributions and clarifies how solidarity is understood in this book. Chapter 3 discusses the significance of different understandings of temporality and why this is crucial to understanding the phenomena of generations. In Chapter 4, a concept of intergenerational solidarity is developed. The book's second part, Chapters 5–8, consists of empirical analyses. Chapter 5 is an analysis of the UN 2030 Agenda with the SDGs, Chapter 6 analyses national political institutions for future generations, Chapter 7 examines national constitutions with protection clauses for future generations, and Chapter 8 studies regulations of national economic debt or savings for future generations. Chapter 9 compares the findings and concludes.

References

Anderson, B. (1991). *Imagined communities: Reflections on the origin and spread of nationalism*. Verso.

Andersen, S. (2013). *Casestudier forskningsstrategi, generalisering og forklaring*. Universitetsforlaget.

Asdahl, K., & Reinertsen, H. (2021). *Doing document analysis. A practice-oriented method*. Sage.

Banting, K., & Kymlicka, W. (Eds.) (2017). *The strains of commitment. The political sources of solidarity in diverse societies*. Oxford University Press.

Bazzani, G. (2023). Climate solidarity: A framework and research agenda for low-carbon behaviour. *Sociological Forum*, *38*(2), 352–374.

Boston, J. (2021). Protecting long-term interests: The role of institutions as commitment devices. In J. Linehan, & P. Lawrence (Eds.), *Giving future generations a voice: Normative frameworks, institutions and practice* (pp. 86–107). Edward Elgar.

Brown Weiss, E. (2021). The theoretical framework for international legal principle of intergenerational equity and implementation through national institutions. In M.-C. C. Segger, M. Szabo, & A. R. Harrington (Eds.), *Intergenerational justice in sustainable development treaty implementation* (pp. 16–43). *Advancing Future Generations' Rights through National Institutions*. Cambridge University Press.

Büchs, M., & Koch, M. (2017). *Postgrowth and wellbeing: Challenges to sustainable welfare*. Palgrave Macmillan.

Busemeyer, M. (2024). Who cares for the future? Exploring public attitudes towards the needs of future generations in Germany. *Journal of European Public Policy*, *31*(3), 680–705.

Caney, S. (2018). Justice and future generations. *Annual Review of Political Science*, *21*, 475–493.

Davoodi, H. R., Elger, P., Fotiou, A., Garcia-Macia, D., Han, X., Lagerborg, A., Lam, W. R., & Medas, P. A. (2022). Fiscal rules and fiscal councils: Recent trends and performance during the pandemic (*IMF working paper* No. 22/11). International Monetary Fund. https://www.imf.org/en/Publications/WP/Issues/2022/01/21/Fiscal-Rules-and-Fiscal-Councils-512128

Dirth, E. (2018). *A global review of the implementation of intergenerational equity*. Utrecht University Repository. Retrieved 10.11.2023 from https://dspace.library.uu.nl/handle/1874/361333

Dirth, E., & Kormann da Silva, N. (2022). *Building our common future: The role of the network of institutions for future generations in safeguarding the future.* ZOE Institute for Future-fit Economies. Retrieved 06.05.2024 from https://zoe-institut.de/wp-content/uploads/2023/10/Building_Our_Common_Future_ZOE_Report_2022.pdf

Entman, R. M. (1993). Framing: Towards clarification of a fractured paradigm. *Journal of Communication*, *43*(4), 51–58.

Gómez-Franco, I. (2024). Amplified solidarity with future generations. *Philosophies*, *9*(17), 1–4.

Gosseries, A. (2011). Three models of intergenerational reciprocity. In A. Gosseries, & L. H. Meyer (Eds.), *Intergenerational justice* (pp. 119–146). Oxford University Press.

Gosseries, A. (2014). The intergenerational case for constitutional rigidity. *Ratio Juris*, *27*(4), 528–539.

Gosseries, A., & Meyer, L. H. (Eds.) (2011). *Intergenerational justice.* Oxford University Press.

Habermas, J. (2015). *The lure of technocracy.* Polity.

IPCC. (2023). Intergovernmental panel on climate changes. Climate Change 2023. Synthesis Report. Retrieved 12.04.2024 from https://www.ipcc.ch/report/ar6/syr/downloads/report/IPCC_AR6_SYR_FullVolume.pdf

Jakobsen, K. A. (2009). Innledning til verdensborgerskapets idéhistorie. In K. A. Jakobsen (Ed.), *Verdensborgerskapets idéhistorie, Vol. 1: Den vestlige tradisjonen* (pp. 9–52). Unipub forlag.

Jones, N., O'Brien, M., & Ryan, T. (2018). Representation of future generations in United Kingdom policy-making. *Futures*, *102*, 153–163.

Koch, M. (2023). Welfare in degrowth transformations. *The Public Sector*, *49*(2), 19–22.

Lawrence, P. (2014). *Justice for future generations: Climate change and international law.* Edward Elgar.

Lawrence, P. (2022). Justifying representation of future generations and nature: Contradictory or mutually supporting values? *Transnational Environmental Law*, *11*(3), 553–579.

Linehan, J., & Lawrence, P. (Eds.) (2021). *Giving future generations a voice. Normative frameworks, institutions and practice.* Edward Elgar.

MacAskill, W. (2022). *What we owe the future.* Basic Books.

MacKenzie, K. (2021). *Future publics. Democracy, deliberation, and future-regarding collective action.* Oxford University Press.

March, J. G., & Olsen, J. P. (1995). *Democratic governance.* The Free Press.

Maxton, G., & Randers, J. (2016). *Reinventing prosperity.* Greystone Books.

NBIM. (2024). Norges banks investment management. About Us. Retrieved 16.04.2024 from https://www.nbim.no/en/organisation/about-us/

Norwegian Petroleum. (2023). Web page Norwegian Petroleum, The Government's revenues. Retrieved 08.08.2023 from https://www.norskpetroleum.no/en/economy/governments-revenues/

Norwegian Petroleum. (2024). Exports of oil and gas. Retrieved 16.04.2024 from https://www.norskpetroleum.no/en/production-and-exports/exports-of-oil-and-gas/

Pascual, U., Balvanera, P., Anderson, C. B., Chaplin-Kramer, R., Christie, M., González-Jiménez, D., Martin, A., Raymond, C.M., Termansen, M., Vatn, A., Athayde, S., Baptiste, B., Barton, D.N., Jacobs, S., Kelemen, E., Kumar, R., Lazos, E., Mwampamba, T.H., Nakangu, B., ... Zent, E. (2023). Diverse values of nature for sustainability. *Nature*, 620, 813–823.

Rawls, J. (1971). *A theory of justice.* Harvard University Press.

Rawls, J. (2001). *Justice as fairness. A restatement.* Harvard University Press.

Schoyen, M. A., Koch, M., & Takle, M. (2022). Partially institutionalized eco-social policymaking in Germany. In M. A. Schoyen, B. Hvinden, & M. D. Leiren (Eds.), *Towards sustainable welfare states in Europe. Social policy and climate change* (pp. 109–130). Edward Elgar.

Schoyen, M. A., & Takle, M. (2022). The Norwegian sustainability paradox: Leader abroad, laggard at home. In M. A. Schoyen, B. Hvinden, & M. D. Leiren (Eds.), *Towards sustainable welfare states in Europe. Social policy and climate change* (pp. 153–174). Edward Elgar.

Segger, M.-C. C., Szabo, M., & Harrington, A. R. (Eds.) (2021). *Intergenerational justice in sustainable development treaty implementation. Advancing future generations' rights through national institutions*. Cambridge University Press.

Setzer, J., & Higham, C. (2022). Global Trends in Climate Change Litigation: 2022 Snapshot. Retrieved 11.05.2023 from https://www.lse.ac.uk/granthaminstitute/publication/global-trends-in-climate-change-litigation-2022/

Setzer, J., & Higham, C. (2023). Global Trends in Climate Change Litigation: 2023 Snapshot. Retrieved 24.04.2024 from https://www.lse.ac.uk/granthaminstitute/wp-content/uploads/2023/06/Global_trends_in_climate_change_litigation_2023_snapshot.pdf

Smith, G. (2021). *Can democracy safeguard the future?* Polity Press.

Statista (2023) Das Statistik Portal. Vergleich der aus Russland importierten Gasmenge mit den gesamten deutschen Gasimporten von 2011 bis 2021. Retrieved 27.10.2023 from https://de.statista.com/statistik/daten/studie/1302674/umfrage/russischer-anteil-am-deutschen-gasimport/

Stjernø, S. (2005). *Solidarity in Europe: The history of an idea*. Cambridge University Press.

Takle, M. (2021a). Common concern for the global ecological commons: Solidarity with future generations? *International Relations*, *35*(3), 403–421.

Takle, M. (2021b). Solidarity with future generations? Protection clauses in constitutions. In A. Falch-Eriksen, M. Takle, & B. Slagsvold (Eds.), *Generational tensions and solidarity within advanced welfare states* (pp. 59–72). Routledge.

Takle, M. (2021c). The Norwegian petroleum fund: Savings for future generations? *Environmental Values*, *30*(2), 147–167.

Takle, M. (2023). Citizenship for future generations: The inclusion of future generations in welfare state considerations. In M. Takle, J. S. Vedeler, M. Schoyen, K. Klette-Bøhler, & A. Falch-Eriksen (Eds.), *Citizenship and social exclusion at the margins of the welfare state* (pp. 108–121). Routledge.

Thiery, W., Lange, S., Rogelj, J., Schleussner, C-F., Gudmundsson, L., Seneviratne, S.I., Andrijevic, M., Frieler, K., Emanuel, K., Geiger, T., Bresch, D.N., Zhao, F., Willner, S.N., Büchner, M., Volkholz, J., Bauer, N., Chang, J., Ciais, P., Dury, M., ... Wada, Y. (2021). Intergenerational inequities in exposure to climate extremes. Young generations are severely threatened by climate change. *Science*, *374*(6564), 158–160. https://doi.org/10.1126/science.abi7339

Thunberg, G. (Ed.) (2022). *The climate book*. Allen Lane.

Tong, S., Samet, J. M., Steffen, W., Kinney, P. L., & Frumkin, H. (2023). Solidarity for the Anthropocene. *Environmental Research*, *235*, 116716. https://www.sciencedirect.com/science/article/abs/pii/S0013935123015207?via%3Dihub

Tremmel, J. (2006). Establishing intergenerational justice in national constitutions. In J. Tremmel (Ed.), *Handbook of intergenerational justice* (pp. 187–214). Edward Elgar.

Tremmel, J. (2009). *A theory of intergenerational justice*. Earthscan.

Tremmel, J. (2015). Parliaments and future generations: The four-power model. In D. Birnbacher, & M. Thorseth (Eds.), *The politics of sustainability. Philosophical perspectives* (pp. 212–233). Routledge.

Tremmel, J. (2021). The four-branches model of government: Representing future generations. In M.-C. C. Segger, M. Szabo, & A. R. Harrington (Eds.), *Intergenerational justice in sustainable development treaty implementation. Advancing future generations rights through national institutions* (pp. 754–780). Cambridge University Press.

UN 2030 Agenda. (2015). Transforming our world: The 2030 agenda for sustainable development. Resolution adopted by the General Assembly on 25 September 2015. Retrieved 24.04.2024 from https://documents.un.org/doc/undoc/gen/n15/291/89/pdf/n1529189.pdf?token=pi8KVlOSHwSRbar7mV&fe=true

UNEP. (2023). SEI, Climate Analytics, E3G, IISD, and UNEP. Phasing Down or Phasing Up? Top Fossil Fuel Producers Plan Even More Extraction Despite Climate Promises: Production Gap Report 2023. https://doi.org/10.51414/sei2023.050

UN Earth Summit in Rio de Janeiro. (1992). United Nations framework convention on climate change. Earth Summit in Rio de Janeiro. Retrieved 02.03.2024 from https://unfccc.int/resource/docs/convkp/conveng.pdf

UN General Assembly. (2020). UN General Assembly. Human Rights Council, Forty-Third Session, 24 February–20 March 2020 Agenda item 3. Visit to Norway. Retrieved 24.04.2024 from https://www.nhri.no/wp-content/uploads/2020/03/Rapport-fra-FNs-spesialrapportør-for-miljø-2020.doc.pdf

UN Policy Brief. (2023). To think and act for future generations. Retrieved 17.01.2024 from https://www.un.org/sites/un2.un.org/files/our-common-agenda-policy-brief-future-generations-en.pdf

WCED. (1987). World commission on environment and development. Our common future. Retrieved 24.04.2024 from http://www.un-documents.net/our-common-future.pdf

Wiertz, T., Kuhn, L., & Mattissek, A. (2023). A turn to geopolitics: Shifts in the German energy transition discourse in light of Russia's war against Ukraine. *Energy Research & Social Science*, *98*, 103036. https://doi.org/10.1016/j.erss.2023.103036

PART I

Solidarity in Theory

2

WHAT IS SOLIDARITY?

Introduction

While there is no universally accepted, standard definition of solidarity, some core ideas indicate what the concept entails. Solidarity is based on equality between members of a community. Solidarity should, therefore, be distinguished from charity or care because these are based on hierarchical and vertical relationships between individuals and can be understood in terms of morality (Habermas, 2015). Furthermore, solidarity is based on the idea that equal individuals should support one another to achieve something collectively and that no one should be left behind or disadvantaged (Lynch et al., 2018).

Solidarity can take many forms, such as emotional or financial support or collective actions to solve common social, economic, or political issues. Moreover, solidarity is often associated with classes, religious groups, social movements, and local communities, where individuals meet and work together for a common cause or to promote social justice (Lynch et al., 2018). We can also find solidarity on a macro level in society, such as the nation state, where people imagine a sense of community (Anderson, 1991).

This book examines macro-level solidarity, mainly at the national level, and it discusses how solidarity can be extended to the global level and across generations. At the macro level, where people do not meet face to face, solidarity requires a willingness to institutionalise collective action.

The first section of this chapter presents the two dimensions of solidarity, and the second section discusses how solidarity is a project for change. The third section considers what distinguishes solidarity from justice. The fourth section elaborates on the relations between solidarity and constitutions, the fifth discusses how social norms and practices are inherent in

DOI: 10.4324/9781003400806-3
This chapter has been made available under a CC-BY-NC-ND 4.0 license.

solidarity, and the sixth discusses what solidarity can mean in diverse societies. The final section reflects upon the relations between nation states and cosmopolitanism.

Two core dimensions of solidarity

This book makes a distinction between two dimensions of solidarity, that, in combination, constitute the concept of solidarity. The first dimension consists of ideas, attitudes, and motivation. These concern reciprocity and mutual obligations among equal individuals with shared values, goals, or interests (Stjernø, 2005). Reciprocity presupposes a community that lasts over a certain period. Those who contribute to the community will change over time, and nobody knows what obligations will arise, as this depends on what is required to achieve something collectively. Such ideas are expressed in commitments in the form of laws, political agreements, and declarations.

The second dimension of solidarity is a willingness to establish institutional bindings as one form of collective action. Dependent on their strength, institutional bindings put constraints on political actors to follow an agreed course of action or agreed norms or rules. They are the implementation of commitments in practice. These bindings can be amendments of existing institutions or the establishment of new institutions. While there are legal and political institutions ensuring that the commitments are realised in practice at the national level, there are no corresponding global institutions. Institutions at the global level comprise the UN, human rights institutions, the International Court of Justice, the European Court of Human Rights, and the UN 2030 Agenda.

Solidarity implies that people agree on social norms and practices that are ensured and maintained through legal and political institutions. Both dimensions must thus be fulfilled to show social solidarity.

By applying these two solidarity dimensions, we simultaneously emphasise the institutions' role in shaping solidarity at the macro level. In this regard, we can draw on an institutional approach to public policy processes (Hill, 2013). The institutionalist approach of March and Olsen (1995) is useful in the way they use the term institution both for ideas (e.g. the idea of a government and a parliament) and for the concrete, practical organisation according to the ideas (e.g. what we know as the government and parliament in Norway and Germany). Institutions consist of a meaning structure, which explains and justifies the rules of conduct, and a resource structure, which makes it possible to act according to the rules (March & Olsen, 1995). While the meaning structure governs and legitimises the practice in the institution, the resource structure consists of houses, equipment, people and, not least, budgets (Olsen, 2007).

Accordingly, in analyses of solidarity at the macro level the meaning structure refers to social norms of reciprocity and mutual obligations among equal individuals with shared values, goals, or interests, while the resource structure is a willingness to enter collective binding obligations realised through the amendments or establishment of new formal institutional structures. The dimensions are realised in several different combinations, which take different forms depending on the context of solidarity and the involved actors' understanding. However, analyses of more dramatic changes in public policy also require attention to the country context in which the institutions exist (Hill, 2013), and we return to this in Chapter 4.

The following sections discuss central themes in the literature on solidarity, and theories about the social norms and political processes form the relationship between the two dimensions.

Solidarity as a project for change

Appeals for solidarity are a call for change in situations where there is a lack of trust, unfair shares of responsibility or if there are inequalities. Habermas (2015) discusses this theme in order to obtain European solidarity. He highlights the need to fulfil two dimensions. One is that solidarity exists within the framework of what he calls a political context of life, which in practice is a political community. The other is trust in a form of reciprocity, guaranteed through legally organised relationships (Habermas, 2015). Solidarity is a political concept that requires political and legal institutions.

Habermas has a discourse-theoretical approach to solidarity. He emphasises how solidarity refers to the capacity of persons to form and sustain meaningful intersubjective connections with one another as the basis for their mutual communicative actions. In Habermas' (1997, 2015) terminology, the range of connection from the level of lifeworld communication is transferred to that of the political system based on deliberative institutions. Solidarity is therefore rooted in the capacity of individuals to coordinate their attitudes and actions through a range of reciprocal relationships.

Moreover, Habermas (2015) argues explicitly that appeals for solidarity concern correcting a disorder or injustice within the framework of a political order. He emphasises this argument, especially in connection with the European Union (EU), which he sees as a bearer of post-national solidarity and a vehicle for cosmopolitan ideas and solidarity. Habermas' concept of solidarity can be both national and post-national. The underlying social norm is that solidarity is something that is aimed at, something that must be achieved but is not fully there. The call for solidarity is a response to something missing and a call for action to rectify this situation. It has a forward-looking character.

What distinguishes solidarity from justice?

Solidarity entails more substantial obligations than justice. Habermas' (2015) political concept of solidarity offers a theoretical basis for this argument. More specifically, Habermas (2015, pp. 3–28) defines solidarity by delineating the concept from other related concepts. He argues that solidarity must be distinguished from justice, both in its moral and legal meaning. Moral and legal norms are perceived as "just" when they regulate practices that are in the equal interest of all affected. This means that the obligation to show solidarity must be distinguished from both moral and legal obligations. While moral commands should be obeyed out of respect for the underlying norm itself, the citizen's obedience to the law is conditioned by the sanctioning power of the state ensuring general compliance (Habermas, 2015).

Solidarity is more comprehensive than justice, Habermas argues. When he defines what this *more* can be, he argues that solidarity is related to *Sittlichkeit* or ethical life. He exemplifies this with reference to family ties, which presuppose mutual commitments that go beyond what one would be obligated to either by morality or by law. Ethical obligations are rooted in the bonds of a pre-existing community. In families or other communities based on *Sittlichkeit*, the motivation for mutual obligations will be based on the trust in this reciprocity over time. Habermas (2015) assumes that the confidence in this reciprocity over time means the ethical obligations coincide with the actors' medium- or long-term interests.

Habermas (2015) also delineates solidarity from ethical obligations, as these are rooted in ties of antecedent-existing communities, as we can find in family ties. He argues that solidarity cannot rely on pre-political communities. He has a modern concept of politics. As we return to in Chapter 3, national traditions are often based on ideas of a common ancestry originating from pre-modern ethnic identities and traditions (Smith, 1995). At the nation state level, Habermas (2015) thinks nationalism obscures this distinction between pre-political communities and solidarity as a political concept. Habermas is critical of emphasising the importance of such pre-political historical traditions for today's national political community. In contrast, solidarity presupposes political contexts of life that rest on a legal framework. Habermas (2015) thus defines solidarity as a concept linked to legally organised political communities. These can be at different levels, and, in our context, we discuss national and cosmopolitical solidarity.

Solidarity and constitutions

Constitutions are meant to place certain questions beyond the reach of a simple majority. Most written constitutions are difficult to change, as they often require legislative supermajorities, concurrent majorities of different legislative houses, and/or legislative majorities in two consecutive parliaments (Tremmel, 2017). Such bindings are decisive for solidarity as a guarantee of confidence in reciprocity and maintaining mutual obligations over time. This presupposes a political context of life, which in the contemporary world is in nation states.

The way in which Habermas (1997) references the notion of constitutional patriotism in several contexts may help us understand the political foundation for solidarity. Constitutional patriotism refers to a shared attachment to universalistic principles, such as human rights and popular sovereignty, which are inherent in the idea of constitutional democracy. His argument is that "democratic citizenship need not be rooted in the national identity of a people. However, regardless of the diversity of different forms of life, it does require that every citizen be socialised into a common political culture" (Habermas, 1997, p. 500). The political culture was formed within the framework of the historically established nation states and the national consciousness (Habermas, 2015). Therefore, constitutional patriotism presupposes that national institutions enforce these universal principles.

To explain why solidarity has become a principle of social order in the modern state, it is fruitful to supplement Habermas' approach with discussions of how Preuss (1999) understands solidarity. In common with Habermas, Preuss (1999) argues that solidarity is a modern concept which is not based on pre-political communities. He contends that the concept of solidarity unites two forms of relations among people: *Gemeinschaft* and *Gesellschaft*. This distinction is based on Tönnies' concepts which can be translated as community and society (Preuss, 1999). On the one hand, solidarity includes duties of care nurtured in *Gemeinschaft*-like types of communities such as families. The relations are based on a feeling of sympathy among members. On the other hand, these duties are directed towards people who do not meet face to face and are implemented in *Gesellschaft*-like kinds of communities based on modern institutions. Solidarity can thus be understood as institutionalised reciprocity which combines feelings of sympathy in line with *Gemeinschaft*-like types of communities with modern institutions based on *Gesellschaft*-like kinds of communities (Preuss, 1999).

This combination is enshrined in the institutions of contemporary nation states. Within nation states, rights and duties are mediated through state institutions, which are bound by the basic principles of constitutionalism (Preuss, 1999). The most important principles are legal rights and the connected concepts of an independent judiciary, the separation of powers, and equality before the law. These principles are based on the idea that all forms of governmental power, also a majority in the parliament, are subject to important substantive limitations. The main point is that the constitution places restrictions on the powers of the legislature to preserve the fundamental freedoms of individuals.

Social norms and practices

To understand solidarity among contemporaries, we need to explore in more detail which social norms and practices motivate people to act in solidarity. We thereby turn to how Stjernø (2005, 2015) has usefully traced the way the concept of solidarity has been used in three significant traditions of European thinking: classical sociology, socialist theory, and Christian social ethics. More precisely, he studies the history of the idea of solidarity, and how it is expressed with different words or functional equivalents such as fraternity, brotherhood, unity, and community. Against this background, Stjernø argues that concepts and words must be understood in the light of the conceptual, political, and historical contexts they appear. He shows this in practice through empirical studies of documents from political parties in Western Europe in the late nineteenth century and the twentieth century.

Stjernø draws attention to political actors' willingness to impose political bindings on themselves. His main concern is the establishment and change of specific institutionalised political concepts of solidarity, and this concern is reflected in how he defines solidarity. "Solidarity implies a readiness for collective action and a will to institutionalise that collective action through the establishment of rights and citizenship" (Stjernø, 2005, p. 2). He distinguishes between four dimensions of the concept of solidarity: the foundation of solidarity, the objective of solidarity, the boundaries of solidarity, and the collective orientation.

By conducting empirical studies of political parties in Western Europe, Stjernø (2005) shows how various combinations of these dimensions have created different forms of solidarity throughout history. He concludes that the various form combinations depend on the context and the actors involved. Stjernø (2005) developed his concept of solidarity through historical observations of how solidarity was built and institutionalised in the nineteenth century during the transition to industrial society, and in the twentieth century when relatively stable and homogeneous nation states were established in Europe.

Solidarity in diverse societies

How can a concept of solidarity be defined and adapted to the culturally diverse societies of the twenty-first century? To answer this question, it is useful to turn to how Banting and Kymlicka (2017) develop and apply a concept of solidarity adapted to today's diverse societies. Their point of departure is their observation of a general worry about the impact of ethnic and religious diversity on solidarity. They take a normative stance and explore the potential sources of support for inclusive solidarity. Their initial question is: "What types of political communities, political agents and political institutions and policies serve to sustain solidarity in contexts of diversity?" (Banting & Kymlicka, 2017, p. 2).

Banting and Kymlicka (2017) define solidarity as two key features. The first is a set of attitudes and motivations, while the second concentrates on national solidarity. Regarding the first key feature, they emphasise attitudes of mutual acceptance, cooperation, and mutual support in time of need. Moreover, they emphasise that the need for mutual obligations towards fellow citizens is critical in times of growing diversity. This aligns with Habermas' and Stjernø's belief that neither self-interest nor justice is sufficient to maintain solidarity in a modern society.

The second key feature of Banting and Kymlicka's solidarity concept concentrates on national solidarity. They define themselves in the well-known tradition of Emile Durkheim, who pointed to solidarity as the glue that binds society together and prevents it from disintegrating. The two authors emphasise the importance of studying national solidarity in contrast to the many solidarity studies which have focused on local communities, social movements, and marginalised groups. Banting and Kymlicka (2017) perceive solidarity as a set of attitudes consisting of mutual concern and obligations people have as members of a society. These attitudes appeal to an image of a decent, good, or just society and are rooted in an ethic of membership (Banting & Kymlicka, 2017).

The two authors explicitly avoid the debate about whether this way of understanding solidarity could be cosmopolitan and thus applied to all humans. They only point to the fact that all existing welfare states build on bounded national solidarity. Moreover, they argue that bounded solidarity is needed to "motivate people to accept obligations beyond duties of rescue and humanitarian needs" (Banting & Kymlicka, 2017, p. 6). They may be correct in this, but it is not sufficient for understanding the challenges in today's world, where nation states face challenges they cannot solve alone. Regional and global challenges make it necessary to explore how a concept of solidarity can be developed across space and beyond current time. In this connection, Brunkhorst (2005) discusses whether democratic solidarity is a sufficient concept to apply at the level of global society. His main argument is that there will be no global solidarity without developing democratic self-governance beyond the nation state. This should be developed within a global community under the law (Brunkhorst, 2005).

A challenge to these theoretical contributions is that they hardly discuss the interaction between environmental limitations and social conditions. As Vetlesen (2019) shows, for example, central works by Habermas overlook nature-related as opposed to society-related aspects of capitalist modernity. Vetlesen's point is that the economy is a subsystem of the ecosystem, and that the ecosystem is finite. The pattern of scarcity has changed from man-made to natural capital (Vetlesen, 2019). The same applies to the other theoretical contributions discussed earlier. Such a neglect of environmental conditions is insufficient to understand today's societal development. Ecological destruction, the scarcity of nature, and nature as the basis for all human activity are essential premises for this book's proposal for a concept of solidarity with future generations in Chapter 4.

Nation states and cosmopolitanism

Nation states are the most important political units in the contemporary world. They form how we think and talk about the world, as made up of sovereign nation states and the relations among them as international relations (Calhoun, 1997). The notion of sovereign states can be dated back to the mid-seventeenth century with the creation of the Westphalian order. This order established a principle for how states relate to each other. Nationalism that emerged in the eighteenth and nineteenth centuries worldwide strengthened the internal collective identity of the states and reinforced the divisions between them externally (Elias, 1989). The Westphalian political order, in combination with nationalism, forms the basis of current international relations.

This political order is challenged by global processes, including fast-paced international trade and financial exchanges as well as new communication technology that transfers information in real time. Networks between people and cultures are spreading and becoming ever faster and broader. These processes do not represent fundamental changes but can instead be understood as more of the same and at a faster speed. They build on an understanding that we live in a world society where closed, demarcated political units are impossible. This involves global interactions and trade, which is not a new phenomenon (Beck, 2006).

According to Jakobsen (2009), two characteristics of globalisation form the unique experience of our time, which are essential for understanding how the global Westphalian order is being challenged. Firstly, it means that the borders of the nation states are perforated, as new challenges cut across national borders and must be solved globally. Secondly, new supranational institutions, laws, and agreements are created above the nation states. They intend to coordinate political processes globally and undermine the nation states' sovereignty (Jakobsen, 2009).

These two characteristics are decisive for contemporary discussions about cosmopolitanism. Many scholarly contributions that advance cosmopolitan ideas can be seen as the normative responses to these challenges of globalisation (Beck, 2006; Habermas, 2008; Held, 2010; Jakobsen, 2009). Cosmopolitanism is an idea linked to the Greek word *kosmopolitēs* which means "citizen of the world." The basic idea is that moral obligations are based on humanity and independent of race, gender, nationality, ethnicity, culture, religion, political affiliation, or state citizenship (Brown & Held, 2010). Moreover, these ideas imply that individuals should be united in one single community. Various versions of cosmopolitanism envision this community differently, some focusing on political institutions, others on moral norms or relationships.

Since the Second World War, cosmopolitanism has reflected normative ideas about how to implement new supranational institutions to supplement or replace the Westphalian order of sovereign states. This often means reforming the world's political order so that states and other political units are brought under the authority of supranational agencies (Beitz, 2010). The most apparent cosmopolitan institutions were mentioned earlier: the UN, human rights institutions, and the International Court of Justice. They show that we have duties towards people outside the historically based nation state borders. In Europe, individuals can bring their states to the European Court of Human Rights for human rights violations as enshrined in the European Convention on Human Rights. One example at the regional level is the EU, which is a supranational union where EU law precedes national legislation.

Nation state politics and cosmopolitanism are two normative ideas of how to respond to contemporary challenges based on different understandings of solidarity. According to the ideal type, national solidarity is based on identification and reciprocity among equal citizens within a nationwide society. This kind of solidarity is based on an objective of national unity and well-being for citizens within a bounded community. The boundaries of national solidarity distinguish all citizens in the nation state from others. National solidarity has a strong collective orientation based on ideals of self-imposed bindings through constitutions.

According to the ideal type, cosmopolitan solidarity is based on universal identification and reciprocity among equal people in the world. Solidarity includes all individuals, and the objective is to create a good society or world for everyone. There are no boundaries, and cosmopolitan solidarity encompasses all human beings. Cosmopolitan solidarity has a weak collective orientation built on ideals of justice among people based on human rights and supranational institutions (Takle, 2018).

In practice national and cosmopolitan solidarity often appear simultaneously and in various combinations. By investigating how national politics and cosmopolitanism are combined in practice, we might reveal something new about today's challenges, and horizons for future thinking.

Summary

- Solidarity is defined in terms of a distinction between two dimensions of solidarity, that, in combination, constitute the concept of solidarity.
- The first dimension is ideas of reciprocity and mutual obligations among equal individuals with shared values, goals, or interests.
- The second dimension is a willingness to enter collective binding obligations through formal institutions.
- These dimensions reflect the relations between meaning structure and ideals on the one hand and resource structure and practice on the other.
- Appeals for solidarity are calls for change in situations where there is a lack of trust, unfair shares of responsibility or if there are inequalities.

- Solidarity is more comprehensive than justice and presupposes political contexts of life that are legally organised.
- Constitutions are decisive for solidarity, as they place restrictions on the powers of the legislative and provide confidence in reciprocity and mutual obligations over time.
- Nation state politics and cosmopolitanism are two normative responses to contemporary global challenges.
- National solidarity is based on identification and reciprocity among equal citizens within a national community.
- Cosmopolitan solidarity is based on universal identification and reciprocity among equal people in the world.

References

Anderson, B. (1991). *Imagined communities: Reflections on the origin and spread of nationalism*. Verso.
Banting, K., & Kymlicka, W. (Eds.) (2017). *The strains of commitment. The political sources of solidarity in diverse societies*. Oxford University Press.
Beck, U. (2006). *Cosmopolitan vision*. Polity Press.
Beitz, C. R. (2010). Justice and international relations. In G. W. Brown, & D. Held (Eds.), *The cosmopolitanism reader* (pp. 85–99). Polity Press.
Brown, G. W., & Held, D. (Eds.) (2010). *The cosmopolitanism reader*. Polity Press.
Brunkhorst, H. (2005). *Solidarity. From civic friendship to a global legal community*. The MIT Press.
Calhoun, C. (1997). *Nationalism*. University of Minnesota Press.
Elias, N. (1989). *Studien über die Deutschen: Machtkämpfe und Habitusentwicklung im 19. und 20. Jahrhundert*. Suhrkamp.
Habermas, J. (2008). *The divided West*. Polity Press.
Habermas, J. (2015). *The lure of technocracy*. Polity Press.
Habermas, J. (1997). *Between facts and norms. Contributions to a discourse theory of law and democracy*. Polity Press.
Held, D. (2010). *Cosmopolitanism. Ideals and realities*. Polity Press.
Hill, M. (2013). *The public policy process*. Pearson.
Jakobsen, K. A. (2009). Innledning til verdensborgerskapets idéhistorie. In K. A. Jakobsen (Ed.), *Verdensborgerskapets idéhistorie, Vol. 1: Den vestlige tradisjonen* (pp. 9–52). Unipub forlag.
Lynch, K., Kalaitzake, M., & Crean, M.. (2018). Research report on conceptualizing European solidarity. SOLIDUS project funded by the EU's Horizon 2020 Research and Innovation Programme. Retrieved 24.04.2024 from https://ec.europa.eu/research/participants/documents/downloadPublic?documentIds=080166e5b8e6ac47&appId=PPGMS
March, J. G., & Olsen, J. P. (1995). *Democratic governance*. The Free Press.
Olsen, J. P. (2007). *Europe in search of political order. An institutional perspective on unity/diversity, citizens/their helpers, democratic design/horizontal drift, and the coexistence of orders*. Oxford University Press.
Preuss, U. K. (1999). National, supranational, and international solidarity. In K. Bayertz (Ed.), *Solidarity* (pp. 281–292). Kluwer Academic Publishers.
Smith, A. D. (1995). *Nation and nationalism in a global era*. Polity Press.
Stjernø, S. (2005). *Solidarity in Europe: The history of an idea*. Cambridge University Press.

Stjernø, S. (2015). Solidarity beyond Europe? In J. Salamon (Ed.), *Solidarity beyond borders: Ethics in a globalising world* (pp. 1–27). Bloomsbury Publishing.

Takle, M. (2018). Is the migration crisis a solidarity crisis? In A. Grimmel (Ed.), *The crisis of the European Union challenges, analyses, solutions* (pp. 116–128). Routledge.

Tremmel, J. (2017). Constitutions as intergenerational contracts: Flexible or fixed? *Intergenerational Justice Review*, *3*(1), 4–17.

Vetlesen, A. J. (2019). Critical theory and the environment. In P. E. Gordon, E. Hammer, & A. Honneth (Eds.), *The Routledge companion to the Frankfurt school* (pp. 471–485). Routledge.

3

TEMPORALITY, NARRATIVES, AND GENERATIONS

Introduction

Rapid climate changes and reduced biodiversity have led to new conceptualisations of the relations between environment, society, and time. In a colloquial way, this is often formulated as we are running out of time or that the future is now. Human impact on the earth's system requires new ways of understanding history to take geological time into account. The argument is linked to the conceptualising of Anthropocene as the geological age: "(....) a time in which human activity has radically altered the planet's climate, atmosphere, biodiversity, chemistry, and geology" (Eriksen et al., 2023, pp. 10–11). Anthropocene is a general term used in many academic disciplines and public debates, and it can thus be seen as an umbrella concept that can be used to raise debates about rapid environmental destruction (Eriksen et al., 2023).

In a broad sense, this book can be placed in this trend where new relationships between time, environmental destruction, and societal changes are discussed. In this book, these relationships are narrowed down to how current generations consider how we leave the world to future generations. It concerns if and how today's generations include the future consequences of contemporary decisions. The time aspect is crucial. It applies to how we relate to the future in the present and how the past sets the conditions for what we do or do not do. This chapter concentrates on how the social organisation of time is associated with territorial and administrative boundaries (Elias, 1988).

This chapter's first section distinguishes between three main understandings of temporality: clock time, event time, and natural time. The second section discusses how narratives are one of our most important ways of organising our perception of time. In the third section, different understandings of temporality

DOI: 10.4324/9781003400806-4
This chapter has been made available under a CC-BY-NC-ND 4.0 license.

and narratives are brought together through the concept of framing. The fourth section discusses nationalism and temporality, and the fifth discusses cosmopolitanism and temporality. The sixth section presents different approaches to studies of generations, and the final section elaborates on how future generations can be combined with these various approaches to generations and argues that future generations should be added to this list of generational studies.

Perceptions of temporality

In the social sciences, temporality refers to the human perception of time and the political and social organisation of time (Kverndokk & Eriksen, 2021). The perception of time refers to various ways of approaching the relationships between past, present, and future. In modern societies, the time of the clock governs our actions. Clock time is a linear time where every second, minute, hour, day, week, month, and year can be counted. Time is homogeneous as every time unit is equal; a minute is always a minute, and one minute relates to the next minute. Clock time is thus called empty or mechanical time (Wyller, 2011). Clock time is continuous, abstract, and universal. It is the same worldwide, and we operate in different time zones. These features make clock time a practical instrument to synchronise people in larger communities than those with whom one has direct contact (Elias, 1988). Clock time is a relatively new invention. The introduction of clock time was decisive for the industrial revolution and the creation of nation states (Gellner, 1983).

While clock time has taught us punctuality and the synchronisation of our actions in modern times, our lives are not guided by the clock alone (Elias, 1988). We also live in a time of events, where events determine our understanding of time. Event time is qualitative. This perception of time is connected to the individual event, as event time is heterogeneous and thus differs depending on the event in question. Events have their own inherent pace, which is different if you, for example, are running to catch a bus or waiting for a bus. Moreover, event time is discrete, concrete, and locally adapted to the particular place where the event takes place (Elias, 1988).

These different perceptions of time are decisive for how we organise ourselves in societies.

Concerning clock time, an external clock determines when a task begins and ends. For example, we have lunch between 1 pm and 2 pm, and the meeting lasts from 2 pm to 3 pm. Based on an event time, tasks will be planned in relation to other tasks, and a task is finished when it is perceived as completed. We eat lunch when we are hungry, and the meeting lasts until the task is completed or the problem is solved. While clock time is important for continuously synchronising people's lives, event time is without a strict timetable.

Event time can be associated with what is called natural time. Natural time follows the rhythm of the sun and the seasons. These rhythms structure time in terms of a regular recurrence. Natural time is circular and based on repetitions, such as the sun's rising and setting each day (Eriksen, 1999).

Temporality in narratives

What are narratives doing for us? Abbott (2015) points out that they do many things, but if we must choose one answer above all others, "narrative is the principal way in which our species organizes its understanding of time" (Abbott, 2015, p. 3). Narratives give us the tools to grasp the world in time, and they give us a frame or a context.

Both clock time and natural time provide a grid of regular intervals. In clock time, these grids are seconds, minutes, hours, etc. In natural time, the grids consist of the passage of the sun, the cycles of the seasons and similar phenomena in nature. Within these grids we can locate events. The grids create the time order, but neither the clock nor natural time organise the narrative. By creating narratives, a sequence is introduced that is linked to events.

The main point is that the narrative can shape time according to human priorities (Abbott, 2015). The narrative creates sequences that are constructed from events and anchored in the grid of clock time or natural time. Through the narrative, we prioritise which events are essential and leave out others of lesser importance. Narrative selects the events that appear as links in a chain.

Narratives shape time as a succession of events, and the events give shape to and dominate our sense of time. We can add greater complexity to the narrative through an accumulation of events. This slows down the narrative time. We can also make narrative time go fast in terms of clock time if, for example, the narrative structure stretches over many years (Abbott, 2015).

In our daily lives, in the public sphere and in politics, we combine various understandings of time. One example from our daily lives is how Kverndokk and Eriksen (2021) study climate change temporalities in vernacular, popular, and scientific discourse. The authors explore a fine-grained system of various time concepts useful for cultural studies such as timescales, time spans, intervals, rhythms, cycles, and changes in accelerations. They discuss how various conceptions of time are helpful for understanding the social and political consequences of climate change (Kverndokk & Eriksen, 2021).

In the public sphere, one example is how Ytterstad and Bødker (2022) show how climate journalists use the green shift to circumvent the challenge that climate change has a long-term horizon and is global. They show how journalism on climate change constructs temporal frames where local events and their temporality are identified and communicated. Borgen-Eide (2024) shows how climate narratives in the media are used to take the reader into climatically changed futures. She shows how narratives connect various possible outcomes to various places and to future generations, thereby bringing social futures to life. In Norway, we find various narratives in the media in which temporality is linked to oil production and the green shift (Borgen-Eide & Ytterstad, 2020).

Regarding politics, Reinhart Koselleck (1989) shows how different understandings of time lie above and below each other as time layers. What he calls historical time arose around the end of the eighteenth century. Historical time is a secular time with a linear direction, like clock time, combined with a narrative. According to Koselleck, the Enlightenment's belief in progress was decisive for the linear form of historical awareness. Through the idea of progress, the circular view of history as repeating the same events was abandoned. Instead, the future became an open horizon for entirely new things to happen. The faith of progress is a modern notion based on historical times. It has had significant impact on modern people's social, political, and economic thinking. Climate change and reduced biodiversity represent a break with the belief in progress.

This new understanding of progress, Koselleck argues, created changes in the understanding of the past. Koselleck's thesis is that an open future leads to a variable past. The meaning of not only the present but also the past is changing as time goes by (Koselleck, 1989). The point is that humans give the past meaning, and the past is not understood as a succession of recurring natural events. History is our present past, and each generation defines its own past. Writing history equals constructing narratives. We give meaning to historical events by inserting them into narratives. We will return to this in discussions of nationalism and temporality.

Framing – selections and salience

These different understandings of temporality and narratives can be brought together in a concept of framing. Framing is an analytical tool that can be used to place short messages into a larger context. The concept of framing refers to people's interpretive schemes for making sense of social reality and motivating them to take various actions (Goffman, 1974).

According to Entman (1993), framing involves selection and salience. Framing is about choosing some items of information over others and making them more salient in terms of more notable, meaningful, and memorable to audiences. Frames call attention to some aspects and obscure others, Entman notes, and the way in which a case is framed can lead to different reactions among audiences.

> To frame is to *select some aspects of a perceived reality and make them more salient in a communicating text, in such a way as to promote a particular problem definition, causal interpretation, moral evaluation, and/or treatment recommendation* for the item described.
>
> *(Entman, 1993, p. 52, emphasis in original)*

This definition of framing is useful as a methodological approach in empirical studies of which narratives are highlighted in different situations, and how time is perceived. Entman emphasises that frames have at least four locations in a communication process. Firstly, communicators use framing judgements to decide what to say. Secondly, the text contains frames which are manifested by keywords, phrases, sources of information, etc. Thirdly, the receiver's thinking may or may not be guided by the same framing intention as communicator and the text. Fourthly, the culture contains the set of common frames in the discourse and thinking of people in a grouping (Entman, 1993).

Different frames arise in different communication contexts. In political studies, for example, analyses of frames can show the background for political decisions and whether new interpretive schemes develop over time (Henningsen & Takle, 2024). As we shall see, this is crucial for how nationalism and cosmopolitanism relate to temporality.

Nationalism and temporality

The introduction of clock time was decisive in organising nation states by making it possible to synchronise people's actions in large communities (Eriksen, 1999). But the national community is also built on narratives, and just as there are many different nation states, the narratives about them differ. Nevertheless, the different national narratives have some common frames.

According to Anderson (1991), the notion of a national community is based on parallelism or simultaneity. In the last quarter of the eighteenth century, the production of watches, serially published newspapers, and novels made it possible to coordinate actions. Anderson (1991) argues that print capitalism made it possible for people to think of themselves as part of a community that lived parallel lives with others. One could be aware of sharing a language, religion, customs, and traditions with others without expecting to meet them. National narrative was built on simultaneous actions in homogeneous, empty, or clock time.

However, Anderson (1991) also emphasises how the national imagination is built on narratives, prioritising events within a homogeneous clock time. In Europe, these narratives are about nations awakening from sleep. The national community rediscovered something deep down, such as language, which created continuity with the past. Nations, like modern persons, Anderson notes, create narratives about a life based on documentary evidence, which show a form of continuity on which one can create an identity. As the past cannot be remembered, it must be narrated. These narratives, like novels and newspapers, are based on historical time (Anderson, 1991).

Similarly, Smith (1995; 2008) emphasises that the central concept to the national myth is that nations have existed since time immemorial and must be revived from a long sleep. He argues that a nation's power lies within this reawakening narrative. Smith (2008) also points to how the significance of particular years is subordinated to the narrative of the nation's origin. Other researchers highlight the nation as an exclusively modern phenomenon that was made possible with industrialisation, modernisation, state formation, the political interest of elites, etc. (Calhoun, 1997). Gellner (1983) rejects the concept that the nation is an awakening of culture, but he shows how nationalism uses historically inherited traditions to justify the nation. When nations refer to inherited traditions, he notes, they do so selectively and often change their traditions radically (Gellner, 1983).

The intention is not to enter the debate about explanations of the origins of nations, but to underscore how nation building selects historical events to create narratives about themselves. National frames are fundamentally retrospective, in which historical traditions form and justify contemporary understandings of national solidarity through narratives.

Cosmopolitanism and temporality

In common with nationalism, cosmopolitanism builds on historical traditions. Cosmopolitanism as a history of ideas originates in ancient Greek and Roman philosophy and early modern Western political thoughts (Jakobsen, 2009). However, contemporary understandings of cosmopolitanism can be seen as normative responses to the current globalisation processes (Beck, 2006; Habermas, 2008; Held, 2010). As discussed in Chapter 2, the uniqueness of our time is linked to how globalisation is understood as processes challenging the Westphalian political order consisting of sovereign nation states (Jakobsen, 2009).

There are different approaches to cosmopolitanism, but like nationalism, cosmopolitanism as a normative idea has some typical frames. These commonalities include temporality, that is, our perception of time and our political and social organisation of time. Cosmopolitanism as a normative response to globalisation refers to processes, which have made the world smaller and more compressed concerning time and space. If we are to highlight one decisive dimension of globalisation important for temporality, it must be that we can experience events in real time. This modern empirical reality presupposes that clock time has made it possible to synchronise actions globally, and in real time. We not only learn about events on the other side of the earth at the same time as they occur, but they often also have direct consequences for our lives, such as a sudden drop in oil price or a rise in price of a particular foodstuff. This emphasis on contemporary global interconnectedness is substantiated by global phenomena such as environmental destruction, pandemics, and financial crises. These processes have accelerated significantly since the beginning of the 1990s because various phenomena have increased in complexity and size (Eriksen, 2016).

While nationalism is basically retrospective, cosmopolitan narratives give priority to events in the present as well as future consequences of current actions. Regarding the present, cosmopolitanism concerns supranational solutions that cross nation states' administrative and territorial organisation and encompass the entire world. The central unit is the individual as "the citizen of the world." In cultural terms, cosmopolitanism breaks with the national community of descent in favour of global associations (Vertovec & Cohen, 2002). Cosmopolitanism lacks the historically rooted bonds that nation states have forged over time (Smith, 1995). This has great significance for the ideas of reciprocity that underlie solidarity and the willingness to enter into binding institutional agreements and laws. Cosmopolitanism has a thinner historical and cultural basis for motivation to act in solidarity.

Cosmopolitanism is often justified as a current solution to future problems. Beck (2006) emphasises, for example, that an increasing awareness of common global risks helps to cultivate a universal belief in a globally shared collective future. This makes, he argues, a cosmopolitan future both possible and necessary (Beck, 2006). Another approach to cosmopolitanism is that today's actions shape future narratives about what the living generations did and, thereby, what memories we who live today create for the future (Horsti, 2019). This corresponds with Koselleck's (1989) terminology, that "the present is the future's past." The activities of contemporary generations create narratives about the past for the individuals of the future.

In a global context, the imperialism of European countries creates a historical backdrop for today's global challenges and ideas of cosmopolitanism. There are historical reasons why the global North creates the most environmental destruction while the global South bears the most immense burden (Gough, 2017; Thunberg, 2022). While there are good reasons to apply cosmopolitan solidarity, the significant inequalities in the world make it difficult to talk about a common "we," as the world's citizens. Global capitalism is no longer centred. The prosperous North American and European countries are still central, but many parallel global circuits exist. China, India, and Brazil are among the world's emerging economies.

Studies of generations

Time ensures that all generations are different and have different challenges. As we have seen in Chapter 1, Thiery et al. (2021) estimate that children born in 2020 will experience a two- to seven-fold increase in extreme events compared with people born in 1960. These estimates are based on well-documented and widely supported knowledge (IPCC, 2023).

These scientific facts highlight a severe threat to the safety of young generations compared to the older generations. Accordingly, Thiery and his colleagues launch the application of a "birth cohort perspective" as a basis for quantifying the differences between how today's older and younger generations are exposed to existential threats. This is launched as an alternative to the "period perspective," which assesses climate change in discrete time windows. By applying a cohort perspective, the authors argue, we can quantify changes in lifetime exposure to climate extremes and compare across generations.

The differences between the birth cohorts have already formed the basis for youth-led climate protests and the initiation of climate lawsuits in recent years. The importance of having a generational approach to societal change is more critical today than ever (Falch-Eriksen & Takle, 2021). This mostly applies to societal changes that result from climate change, but also to how other significant challenges have confronted countries worldwide over the last few decades. Some examples are economic challenges due to financial crises leaving austerity measures, social and demographic developments with an ageing population and increased migration, rising poverty levels and increased economic differences, a deadly pandemic, and wars in Ukraine and the Middle East.

By applying a birth cohort perspective, we follow people who were born simultaneously and examine their challenges throughout their life course. This does not, however, mean that every individual within a birth cohort will experience the same challenges in the same way. On the contrary, some individuals will be more exposed than others, depending, among other things, on where they live and their available resources.

The term *social generations* refers to people born in the same period and who are exposed to the same historical and societal challenges. Mannheim (1952) laid the premises for the studies of social generations with this groundbreaking work. Mannheim (1952) suggests that the best way to appreciate which features of social life result from the existence of generations is to imagine how it would be if one generation lived forever and none replaced it. He used this utopian imagination to show how our society is characterised by how generations follow generations. In short, this implies that new participants in the cultural process emerge while former participants disappear. Members of one generation can participate only in a limited section of the historical process. Transitioning accumulated cultural heritage from one generation to the next is a continuous process (Mannheim, 1952). Because we constantly live as overlapping generations, this transition is hardly visible in everyday political lives.

According to Mannheim's approach, coexistence in time as birth cohorts is insufficient to create a generational awareness that gains significance for societal development. The preconditions to be defined as a social generation in Mannheim's terminology are that people must be born in the same period and be exposed to the same historical and societal challenges. The critical prerequisites to be defined as a social generation are that ties are forged between the members, that they create a generational awareness, and that they participate in the social and intellectual currents of their society. Not all age groups create new collective impulses and formative principles sufficient for themselves and the situation. Not all cohorts can thus be called a social generation (Mannheim, 1952). Moreover, Mannheim argues that each social generation could have different generational units. Each unit is a special response to historical stimulus experienced by all within the social generation, and there might be differences between the units.

Social generations can also be studied in terms of dynamics based on tensions between generations (Connolly, 2019). Many of today's societal changes can be understood by Elias' (1989) theories about generational dynamics. Elias (1989) discussed how tensions between generations arise by opening or closing channels for opportunities for young generations, both regarding life opportunities and the meaning of upward social mobility. Elias investigated how wars, revolutions, economic expansion, or peace affected social processes, which in turn opened or closed opportunities for young generations. He used examples from the Weimar Republic in the 1920s and youth groups in the Federal Republic of Germany in the 1960s and 1970s (Elias, 1989).

Society has changed considerably since Mannheim and Elias wrote about generations. The most significant changes are how the consequences of globalisation, digitisation and environmental destruction have the potential to shape generational awareness in terms of Mannheim's approach, but also conflicts between generations as Elias emphasises. We observe a new "global generation," i.e. birth cohorts that experience global processes similarly (Beck & Beck-Gernsheim, 2009). This may be true to some extent, but these changes will have different meanings for the same cohorts in various parts of the world. Such differences may create different generational awareness. Therefore, key aspects of Mannheim's and Elias' understanding of generations as a phenomenon still lay premises for research on generations (Bristow, 2016; Connolly, 2019). Recent studies have a more refined concept of generations, such as historical and ascriptive generations, kinship generation, and future generations (Falch-Eriksen et al., 2021).

The terms *historical and ascriptive generations* capture those generation types that, for some reason, are labelled. Those providing such a label usually seek out conjoined birth cohorts labelled according to a particular historical period, depicting strong characteristics of the current time or social change (Bristow, 2016). Historical generations can be seen as those that qualify for the test of a generational self-definition and the term has much in common with social generations. One cannot escape from one's historical generation. One cannot escape from one's historical generation, as illustrated by, for example, the lost generation after the First World War and the boomer generation after the Second World War (Slagsvold & Hansen, 2021).

Ascriptive generations are brought together, not by belonging to a social generation and a matter of social change or phenomenon but rather by accidental commonalities. These are birth cohorts which are less defined and do not meet the criteria to be called a social generation. They are often given terms such as Generation X, Z, or Y or Millennials or similar other terms (Bristow, 2016).

The term *kinship generations* involves the community's generational complex into which individuals are born, and at its core is the hierarchical parent-child relationship (Pilcher, 1994). However, kinship denotes more than a biological bond between generations; it also involves the family and social communities where the family is socially rooted (Aarset et al., 2021). Within kinship, an individual has different roles throughout the life course, as a child, youth, adult, and old person. Every individual can belong to a social generation and a kinship generation simultaneously, but the two generational concepts have different connections within the social system.

Whereas social generations are connected to the social roles and phenomena in birth cohorts, kinship generations are connected to community belonging combined with thick trust relationships. Common to both concepts are that generations react to and contribute to shaping societal circumstances as individuals age, but they do so differently. In social generations, each individual remains the same generation as time goes by. In kinship generations, individuals shift roles and identities across generations as they grow older and replace previous generations (Falch-Eriksen et al., 2021). As individuals take on new roles, they simultaneously gain new opportunities to influence societal development.

Future generations in generational studies

In Chapter 1, the concept of future generations is defined as young people living today as well as unborn generations. The relations between young people living today and the current adult generations are ones between overlapping generations.

The concept of future generations can only be combined with these different approaches to generations if generations live simultaneously and can relate to one another as overlapping generations. Defining future generations as unborn people makes it challenging to combine them with the commonly used approaches in generational studies.

As overlapping generations, we can apply Mannheim's terminology to studies of whether future generations have a generational awareness and thereby form a social generation. Based on Elias' concept of conflict between generations, we can study future generations regarding whether the older generation opens or closes opportunities to the young generations. This requires, however, future generations to be understood as young people living today and at the same time as today's old people.

Future generations can be discussed as a historical and ascriptive generation, labelled as the first young generation that grows up with extreme global environmental destruction. Labels like *Fridays for Future Generation*, the *Greta Thunberg Generation*, and the *Last Generation* may reflect key features of an era, but they are not sufficiently precise as analytical tools to understand the role of different generations in societal development. We need empirical research to find out if these are only labels or if the young generation has developed a generational awareness as a social generation.

We can also analyse future generations in terms of kinship, as our children and grandchildren, based on their current societal role without political influence and with adults responsible for their future (Scheffler, 2018). The kinship approach to future generations brings the challenges closer to our lives as they are our children or grandchildren, not simply some unknown future people. The future is perceived as less abstract and more imaginable when it is connected to the current generation of parents' hopes for their descendants (Kverndokk, 2020). It becomes more manageable to understand how our responsibility in the present is to secure these future expectations. Future generations as unborn people are more problematic to study from a kinship approach. The social and moral ties that are linked in kinship are not there. Political rhetoric is often built on moral argumentation drawn from the family sphere. It is easy to gain support for the argument that we must take care of our grandchildren, but not as easy to consider people we do not know and who have not yet been born.

Therefore, future generations should be added to this list of various approaches to generations. However, studies of people who have not yet been born differ from the other approaches to generational studies. In contrast to the currently living young people, the unborn future generations cannot be studied as such. Their lives in the future are a challenge for today's generations. This means that studies of future generations are about the present day. This concerns the current generation's priority of those who are not yet born. Such priorities are contested. Studies of future generations involve a future-oriented mindset that will become more important because young people and those who will be born in the future are increasingly dependent on current political decision-making.

Summary

- In the social sciences, temporality refers to the human perception of time and the political and social organisation of time.
- A narrative is a tool for arranging time, interpreting phenomena and events, and placing them in time.
- Different understandings of temporality and narratives can be brought together in a concept of framing.
- Framing is about choosing some information over other information and making it more salient in terms of more notable, meaningful, and memorable to audiences.

- National ideas are in general retrospective, in which historical traditions form and justify contemporary understandings of national solidarity through narratives.
- Cosmopolitan ideas give priority to events in the present and solutions crossing national administrative and territorial boundaries and encompassing the entire world.
- Cosmopolitanism has a thinner historical and cultural basis for motivation to act in solidarity than national solidarity.
- Generational studies can be divided into social generations, historical and ascriptive generation, and kinship generations.
- Studies of future generations can only be combined with these different approaches to generations if generations live simultaneously and can relate to each other as overlapping generations.
- Studying future generations such as children, grandchildren, great-grandchildren, and unborn people can make the future less abstract as they are people we know will live in a world we leave behind, but unborn people are challenging to describe with family-based terms.
- Studies of people who have not yet been born cannot be done as such in the same way as we study living generations, and studies of future generations concern the priorities of the present day.

References

Aarset, M. F., Smette, I., & Rosten, M. G. (2021). Thinking through generation: On parenting and belonging among adult children of immigrants in Norway. In A. Falch-Eriksen, M. Takle, & B. Slagsvold (Eds.), *Generational tensions and solidarity within advanced welfare States* (pp. 79–95). Routledge.

Abbott, H. P. (2015). *The Cambridge introduction to narrative* (14th ed.). Cambridge University Press.

Anderson, B. (1991). *Imagined communities: Reflections on the origin and spread of nationalism*. Verso.

Beck, U. (2006). *Cosmopolitan vision*. Polity Press.

Beck, U., & Beck-Gernsheim, E. (2009). Global generations and the trap of methodological nationalism for a cosmopolitan turn in the sociology of youth and generation. *European Sociological Review*, *25*(1), 25–36.

Borgen-Eide, G. (2024). Storying climatically changed worlds—Potentials and pitfalls of future journalism. *Journalism Practice*. https://doi.org/10.1080/17512786.2024.2310049

Borgen-Eide, G., & Ytterstad, A. (2020). Dansen rundt den hellige kua. Klimakoblinger i fire kommentarers narrativer om oljekrisepakken i 2020. *Norsk Medietidsskrift*, *30*(3), 1–17.

Bristow, J. (2016). *The sociology of generations: New directions and challenges*. Springer.

Calhoun, C. (1997). *Nationalism*. University of Minnesota Press.

Connolly, J. (2019). Generational conflict and the sociology of generations: Mannheim and Elias reconsidered. *Theory, Culture & Society*, *36*(7–8), 153–172.

Elias, N. (1988). *Arbeiten zur Wissenssoziologie: 2: Über die Zeit*. Suhrkamp.

Elias, N. (1989). *Studien über die Deutschen: Machtkämpfe und Habitusentwicklung im 19. und 20. Jahrhundert*. Suhrkamp.
Entman, R. M. (1993). Framing: Towards clarification of a fractured paradigm. *Journal of Communication*, *43*(4), 51–58.
Eriksen, T. B. (1999). *Tidens historie*. Stenersens forlag.
Eriksen, T. H. (2016). *Overheating. An anthropology of accelerated change*. Pluto Press.
Eriksen, T. H., Schroer, S. A., & Münster, U. (2023). Introduction: Responding to the Anthropocene. In U. Münster, T. H. Eriksen, & S. A. Schoroer (Eds.), *Responding to the Anthropocene. Perspectives from twelve academic disciplines* (pp. 9–33). Scandinavian Academic Press.
Falch-Eriksen, A., & Takle, M. (2021). Generational analysis of the advanced welfare state. In A. Falch-Eriksen, M. Takle, & B. Slagsvold (Eds.), *Generational tensions and solidarity within advanced welfare states* (pp. 203–216). Routledge.
Falch-Eriksen, A., Takle, M., & Slagsvold, B. (2021). *Generational tensions and solidarity within advanced welfare states*. Routledge.
Gellner, E. (1983). *Nations and nationalism. New perspectives on the past*. Blackwell Publishers.
Goffman, E. (1974). *Frame analysis: An essay on the organization of experience*. Northeastern University Press.
Gough, I. (2017). *Heat, greed and human need. Climate change, capitalism and sustainable wellbeing*. Edward Elgar.
Habermas, J. (2008). *The divided West*. Polity Press.
Held, D. (2010). *Cosmopolitanism. Ideals and realities*. Polity Press.
Henningsen, E., & Takle, M.. (2024). Cultural policy and the politics of display. The establishment of the opera house in Oslo. *International Journal of Cultural Policy*. https://doi.org/10.1080/10286632.2024.2333857
Horsti, K. (2019). Temporality in cosmopolitan solidarity: Archival activism and participatory documentary film as mediated witnessing of suffering at Europe's borders. *European Journal of Cultural Studies*, 22(2), 231–244.
IPCC. (2023). Intergovernmental panel on climate changes. Climate change 2023. Synthesis report. Retrieved 12.04.2024 from https://www.ipcc.ch/report/ar6/syr/downloads/report/IPCC_AR6_SYR_FullVolume.pdf
Jakobsen, K. A. (2009). Innledning til verdensborgerskapets idéhistorie. In K. A. Jakobsen (Ed.), *Verdensborgerskapets idéhistorie, Vol. 1: Den vestlige tradisjonen* (pp. 9–52). Unipub forlag.
Koselleck, R. (Ed.) (1989). *Vergangene Zukunft. Zur Semantik geschichtlicher Zeiten*. Suhrkamp.
Kverndokk, K. (2020). Talking about your generation: "Our children" as a trope in climate change discourse. *Ethnologia Europaea*, *50*(1), 145–158.
Kverndokk, K., & Eriksen, A. (2021). Climate change temporalities: Narratives, genres, and tropes. In K. Kverndokk, M. Ruge, & A. Eriksen (Eds.), *Climate change temporalities. Explorations in vernacular, popular and scientific discourse* (pp. 3–14). Routledge.
Mannheim, K. (1952). *Essays on the sociology of knowledge*. Routledge and Kegan Paul Ltd.
Pilcher, J. (1994). Mannheim's sociology of generations: An undervalued legacy. *British Journal of Sociology*, *45*(3), 481–495.
Scheffler, S. (2018). *Why worry about future generations?* Oxford University Press.
Slagsvold, B., & Hansen, T. (2021). The baby-boomer generation: Another breed of elderly people? In A. Falch-Eriksen, M. Takle, & B. Slagsvold (Eds.), *Generational tensions and solidarity within advanced welfare states* (pp. 153–172). Routledge.
Smith, A. D. (1995). *Nation and nationalism in a global era*. Polity Press.
Smith, A. D. (2008). *The cultural foundation of nations, hierarchy, covenant and republic*. Blackwell.

Thiery, W., Lange, S., Rogelj, J., Schleussner, C-F., Gudmundsson, L., Seneviratne, S.I., Andrijevic, M., Frieler, K., Emanuel, K., Geiger, T., Bresch, D.N., Zhao, F., Willner, S.N., Büchner, M., Volkholz, J., Bauer, N., Chang, J., Ciais, P., Dury, M., ... Wada, Y. Thiery, W. (2021). Intergenerational inequities in exposure to climate extremes. Young generations are severely threatened by climate change. *Science*, 374 (6564), 158–160.

Thunberg, G. (Ed.) (2022). *The climate book*. Allen Lane.

Vertovec, S., & Cohen, R. (2002). Introduction: Conceiving cosmopolitanism. In S. Vertovec, & R. Coven (Eds.), *Conceiving cosmopolitanism: Theory, context and practice* (pp. 1–22). Routledge.

Wyller, T. (2011). *Hva er tid?* Universitetsforlaget.

Ytterstad, A., & Bødker, H. (2022). Climate change journalism in Norway—Working with frequency around the "green shift. *Journalism Studies*, *23*(11), 1291–1307.

4

SOLIDARITY WITH FUTURE GENERATIONS

Introduction

This chapter elaborates on how the two dimensions of solidarity can be extended to include future generations. Two questions are raised. Firstly, how can the idea of reciprocity between equal actors within a political community include people who have not yet been born and who cannot give anything back? Secondly, how can we understand the implementation of commitments in practice in the form of self-imposed institutional constraints when there is no equality between the living generations and future people?

The first section discusses the relationship between intergenerational justice and solidarity. The second and third sections elaborate on how the two dimensions of solidarity can be extended to include future people. Finally, in the fourth section the concept of solidarity with future generations is operationalised in the form of three questions regarding what it takes to act in solidarity with future generations. These three questions will be adapted to and will guide the empirical studies in Part II of this book.

Intergenerational justice and solidarity

The current generation's responsibility for future generations is often analysed from the perspective of intergenerational justice. As discussed in Chapter 1, theories of intergenerational justice consider if and how justice can be applied in relations between generations due to the uncertainty about the lives of unborn persons.

The most important uncertainty is that future generations do not exist, and there is no reciprocity between generations. We have little knowledge

DOI: 10.4324/9781003400806-5
This chapter has been made available under a CC-BY-NC-ND 4.0 license.

of how many people will be born in the future, and we do not know the composition of future generations. We know they will have basic needs like nutrition and clean water, but we do not know their preferences. Moreover, we may assume that later generations will know something we cannot know today, and that technological development will transform society (Caney, 2018). There is uncertainty about how many generations we are responsible for in the future (Tremmel, 2021). This remoteness in time makes it difficult to relate to future people as individuals.

The way we deal with such uncertainties has implications for how we understand whether we have obligations to those who come after us, and, if so, the nature and content of these obligations. This is reflected in how the theories of intergenerational justice interpret the uncertainties and draw different normative implications from them (Gosseries & Meyer, 2011). One approach is that we cannot have responsibility for unborn people because we do not know who they are, and we do not even know if they will be born. This is the essence of what is called the non-identity problem (e.g. Parfit, 2017). Although this approach has received much attention in academic debates on intergenerational justice, it is a derailment from the responsibility that arises from contemporary knowledge about how environmental destruction will have consequences for future people (MacKenzie, 2021).

Another theoretical approach contrasting this non-identity problem is a communitarian understanding of intergenerational justice, which emphasises interests and values as members of a group with a shared past and future. To explain why the present generation has responsibilities towards future people, Thompson (2011) highlights the idea of interests which transcend a lifetime. These interests relate to matters that existed before today's individuals were born and will continue to exist after their death. This will also apply to the living generations' posthumous reputation. However, as Thompson (2011) also notes, strong communitarianism emphasises a common identity as the core of a political community, and this is not compatible with today's multicultural nation states and global spread of human rights norms.

As mentioned in the introduction, two contractual approaches within a liberal political tradition are useful for discussing how one generation determines the nature of its responsibilities for future generations. These are Rawls' (1971; 2001) proposal for justice as impartiality and Gosseries' (2011) theories of intergenerational reciprocity. They offer judgements about principles of intergenerational justice, which are useful for developing a concept of solidarity with future generations.

Rawls starts from a theoretical model, where nobody knows to which generation one belongs and where everyone comes together to determine principles for intergenerational justice. Rawls (1971, pp. 284–310) discusses how his theoretical justice model can be transferred to transgenerational relationships. In this model, decisions are made behind what he calls a "veil of ignorance." This is a hypothetical and non-historical situation. His main point is that nobody knows to which generation one belongs and would therefore treat each generation's viewpoint equally. In this hypothetical context, the outcome of a decision is reached in a contractual decision situation (Rawls, 1971). This is a procedural approach to justice, and if the procedure is just, the outcome should also be just.

By applying the hypothetical model of "veil of ignorance" to intergenerational justice, he distinguishes between two stages in societal development for the application of the principle of just savings. While the first stage is the accumulation stage, the second is that people should leave for their descendants at least the equivalent of what they received from the previous generations. Rawls argued that justice does not require people to save for future people, but they should do what is necessary to allow future people to live under just institutions (Rawls, 2001).

Many later discussions have been reactions to Rawls' contribution. He has been criticised for being too vague, switching between multiple models, and using family metaphors. The most fundamental criticism is that Rawls was concerned with how much a generation should save, thereby overlooking the question of what to save (Caney, 2018; Tremmel, 2009). Rawls (1971, p. 288) emphasised that capital did refer not only to "factories and machines, and so on," but also to knowledge and culture and stable political institutions. He did not have environmental intergenerational problems in mind. This is problematic because we can assume that major ecological problems will be passed on to future generations, and these problems will accelerate as time passes. We cannot assume that the next generation will be better off. Even if we follow the procedures from Rawls' hypothetical model, this will not necessarily help us understand what needs to be done today to show solidarity with our descendants.

According to MacKenzie (2021), Rawls has developed a general theory for all generations at all times, and this model is far from what political actors encounter who are constrained by time. An important task is to assess what to do in a concrete context, and then one must know what justice means in a practical context. Moreover, as Kates (2015) argues, Rawls' principles of intergenerational justice based on the original position run directly contrary to the most basic principles of democracy that political power is morally legitimated by the people who are governed by it. Rawls' model concerns choice and not democratic deliberations among participating actors facing concrete problems.

The second contractual approach within the liberal political tradition is justice as reciprocity, seen as a mutual advantage. This is based on symmetrical exchange. All affected are equal, and those who cannot return benefits or detriments are not considered (Tremmel, 2009). Equality does not imply that we should return precisely the same object but something of equal value. But in a strict sense of reciprocity based on equality, no one should be a net beneficiary or net contributor. Reciprocity can be applied to overlapping generations, as far as the young generation can pay back to the older generations. This principle is problematic to apply to unborn people, as they are not able to take part in such equal exchange. Since justice as reciprocity fails to provide adequate justifications for our obligations towards future generations, one solution is thus to think of this as indirect reciprocity (Gosseries, 2011). This will be discussed further ahead.

The main point here is that studies of intergenerational justice are useful for understanding the uncertainties underlying concerns for future generations (Gosseries & Meyer, 2011; Lawrence, 2014; Tremmel, 2009). They propose abstract principles that are useful to guide each generation, but they are insufficient to understand how to consider future generations in today's political decisions in practice. Moreover, theories of intergenerational justice can be useful to prescribe procedures that will lead to a just outcome; if the procedure is just, its outcome will also be just. However, their proposals for abstract intergenerational justice principles or just procedures have a limited function as analytical tools in empirical studies.

The key argument in this book is that a concept of solidarity would be more suitable than intergenerational justice to examine what kinds of binding commitments to collective action a concern for future generations would require. As discussed in Chapter 2, justice is a part of the concept of solidarity and thus crucial for understanding solidarity. However, solidarity is more comprehensive, as it is a political concept that requires a political community and a legal context (Habermas, 2015).

Moreover, this contribution is made against the background that only few studies of future generations discuss the concept solidarity. As mentioned in Chapter 1, the theoretical and philosophical discussions of solidarity with future generations cover normative concepts and principles that are challenging to apply to empirical studies (Bazzani, 2023; Gómez-Francoez, 2024; Tong et al., 2023). One example, which is often referred to in scholarly literature, is the 2013 UN Secretary-General report on intergenerational solidarity and the needs of future generations (UN Secretary-General, 2013). This report discussed how intergenerational solidarity is embedded in the concept of sustainable development, but the solidarity concept is used generically to include community, social cohesion, a sense of unity, etc. and is therefore challenging to use in new studies.

The same applies to scholarly studies which argue normatively that there is a need to act in solidarity with future generations. Bazzani (2023) argues that climate change has created a new global interdependence that requires a new form of climate solidarity as a global and intergenerational prosocial behaviour. He presents four approaches to prosocial behaviour, which include general assessments. Tong et al. (2023) argue similarly that there is a need for solidarity for the Anthropocene. They argue that the global challenges in the Anthropocene are far-reaching, call for extensive, large-scale action, and, therefore, require solidarity to be handled. Gómez-Franco (2024) suggests a concept she calls amplified solidarity with future generations, which explains the current generations' obligations towards the health and quality of life of future generations. She conducts philosophical considerations along five analytical axes covering ethical principles, ideas and facts, social, political and moral dimensions, asymmetric relationships, and lack of reciprocity. She argues normatively that there is a need for a concept of solidarity, but these general assessments lack tools for empirical analyses.

The two-dimensional concept proposed in this book is intended to be both theoretically grounded and empirically applicable. In the following two sections, the two dimensions of solidarity are applied to future generations. Firstly, the idea of reciprocity between equal actors within a political community and, secondly, these actors' willingness to commit themselves to collective, binding constraints through institutions.

First dimension of solidarity: indirect reciprocity

How can we think of solidarity with future generations when the idea of reciprocity is a core dimension of the concept? It is unrealistic to have expectations of reciprocity with people who have not yet been born. The unborn cannot give anything back, and there is no equality between us living today and them.

While direct reciprocity is based on people relating to each other and having a mutual exchange, indirect reciprocity means giving something to a person, but it is not the same person who gives something in return. You do not necessarily know the person who gives you something back. This is common at the macro level, such as nation states, where people do not meet each other face to face but still redistribute resources through welfare schemes.

From a generational perspective, it is helpful to start with how Gosseries (2011) discusses indirect reciprocity. He discusses two types. Firstly, it can take the form of the current generation transferring something of value, which it has received from its ancestors, to its succeeding generation. This could be, for example, stable political institutions or financial resources transferred between generations. Secondly, indirect reciprocity can also go backwards in time, meaning that today's generations give something to their predecessors on the condition that their descendants provide something to themselves. An example of the latter is old-age pensions, which are paid from state revenue and linked to each working generation paying for the elderly's pensions.

Indirect reciprocity can be understood as stewardship of property between generations. Each generation receives from its predecessors and contributes to the later generations, but none of the generations fully owns what it has inherited from the previous generation (Brown Weiss, 1992; Connelly et al., 2012). The inheritance involves the right to use the advantages of property that one generation has, but only for as long as one lives, and it must be passed on to the next generation. An example is fishing quotas, which regulate who can fish and how much fish they can take to ensure the stock is maintained.

However, the argument about the use and advantages of property is highly problematic in relation to fossil fuel because it is not renewable. Any use of fossil fuels reduces the quantity without being renewed unless we wait for millions of years. Used fossil fuels cannot be passed on to the next generation. The idea of converting fossil fuels to financial investments in stocks and bonds overlooks the fact that fossil fuels are not renewable, and that the combustion of fossil fuels means that greenhouse gas emissions are passed on to the next generation. Therefore, all stewardship of fossil fuels must be handled carefully.

Obligations towards dead people might also influence the current generations' relations to future generations. The obligation is not to give back something, but rather the idea of respecting the will of the dead or owing them a debt of gratitude (Anderson, 1991). Another situation might be that previous generations have committed misdeeds for which today's generations have to make amends. As discussed in Chapter 3, these forms of retrospection are essential to national discussions about what should be handed down further to future generations.

Indirect reciprocity between generations faces a number of challenges. The starting point for reciprocity is that there should be equality between generations, but in situations of indirect reciprocity, it is problematic to decide whether someone wins or loses from the exchange. The future is open and highly uncertain, so it is problematic to decide whether reciprocity leads to equality between the generations involved, that is, whether the current generations transfer as much value to the next generation as they received from the previous generation (Gosseries, 2011). The exchange rate can also be influenced by external factors, for example the value of debt or savings transferred between generations can change. Moreover, projections show that the global population is expected to reach 10.4 billion people by 2100, which means that future generations will be more numerous and must share the same resources as today's generations (UN World Population Prospects, 2022). There is much evidence that future generations will be exposed to the consequences of extreme weather to a much greater extent than today's generations (Thiery et al., 2021 et al., 2021).

Regarding the idea that future generations should not be worse off than the present generation, Tremmel's (2009) contribution is interesting. He calls this "intergenerational justice as enabling advancement." His point of departure is that it is just to make improvement possible for future generations. He emphasises the importance of opportunities for future generations, and these are based on what future people will need, not their preferences. Moreover, Tremmel (2009) compares two subsequent generations. He argues that "If every 'next generation' receives and hands over its inheritance in the sense of indirect reciprocity, this will create a chain of obligations that ultimately affect all future generations" (Tremmel, 2009, p. 199). His argument is that favouring comparisons between two generations will simultaneously maintain the view that we have obligations to all future generations.

In contrast to the calculation that everyone should get back what they invested, the element of calculation in indirect reciprocity is intertwined with the participation and maintenance of a political community (Heath, 2013). In a political community of solidarity, people agree on social norms and practices that are ensured and maintained through legal and political institutions.

What should today's generations provide for future generations through indirect reciprocity? Does indirect reciprocity mean that today's generations should pass on an inheritance to ensure that future people can shape their own lives? Or, formulated in another way, to what extent should today's generations decide what forms the basis for a good future society? These questions concern whether today's generations should facilitate future generations' opportunities to cover basic needs or whether they should get opportunities to develop their own capabilities.

To elaborate on these questions, we can draw on insight from two theoretical approaches. Sen's (2009; 2013) capabilities approach and Gough's (2017) theory on universal human needs. Sen's point of departure is sustainable development as defined by the UN World Commission on Environment and Development (WCED) report. As we have seen in Chapter 1, this is defined as "development that meets the need of the present without compromising the ability of future generations to meet their own needs" (WCED, 1987, Chapter 2, No. 1). He criticises its emphasis on conserving the ability of each generation to meet its respective needs. In contrast, Sen (2013) proposes a freedom-oriented view that focuses on enhancing human capability. One central concern for Sen (2013) is that we see human beings as agents who can think and act, not just as patients who focus on satisfying their needs. This means each generation should be given the freedom and possibility to evaluate and identify its own desires.

Gough (2017) asserts that Sen's capability approach is difficult to operationalise, leaving scant protection for future generations. His essential premise is that all individuals worldwide have specific basic common needs, which must be met to avoid harm, participate in society, and reflect critically. Gough (2017) argues that needs should be given priority over preferences as they imply ethical obligations to individuals and claims of justice on social institutions. This way of defining universal needs makes it, according to Gough (2017), possible to plan for and measure progress towards social and environmental goals. Even though needs might be defined universally, they are satisfied differently across cultures and time. To solve this theoretically, Gough (2017) introduces a form of procedural rationality to identify need satisfiers adapted to particular social settings.

Moreover, climate change is global, long-term, persistent, and cumulative. Therefore, it not only confronts social policy with a qualitative new agenda but will also make pursuing economic and social needs and rights more difficult. Gough (2017) argues that climate change is *the* global threat posing existential danger, which is challenging to coordinate globally. However, climate policy alone could be unjust and inequitable, and it must be combined with the pursuit of sustainable well-being for all current people and future generations (Gough, 2017).

The two approaches to how today's generations give future generations opportunities to meet their needs or develop their capabilities are not mutually exclusive, as they refer to problems of a different nature. Gough refers to a minimum standard. This involves restrictions on, for example, resource use, emissions of greenhouse gases, and biological diversity. This is the prerequisite for getting into the situation Sen believes current generations must create for future generations. Sen's approach is close to the uncertainty inherent in the transfer of inheritance, stewardship role, and responsibility. Indirect reciprocity must take uncertainty into account as this is crucial to cover future generations' needs and capabilities. This implies creating and maintaining political institutions that can stabilise a system based on uncertainty.

Second dimension of solidarity: institutional constraints

The second dimension of solidarity is the willingness to establish collective binding constraints through institutions. This aligns with a core dimension of Stjernø's (2005; 2015) conception of solidarity, namely the strength of collective orientation. He defines this as a question of the extent to which solidarity implies that the actors (individuals or states) should relinquish autonomy and freedom to achieve collective interests or values. Moreover, he distinguishes between strong and weak collective orientation (Stjernø, 2005). By applying this to future generations, we may assume that the collective orientation is weak because the uncertainty about the future is high. For such self-imposed restrictions to be binding, it must be challenging to act against them. One example is constitutions, which, in many countries, require a qualified majority in elected bodies to be changed. The main point is that institutional design is crucial.

One can distinguish between at least two approaches to assess the impact of institutional design (Olsen, 1997; 2007). One approach is to evaluate institutional design based on how it contributes to an institution's immediate substantive result. The decisive factor is the effectiveness of alternative design forms in specific situations. The political actors search for the organisational tools best suited to serve a given set of goals in an efficient way (Goodin, 1996). Design is based on what outcome political actors want from an institution, i.e. what the institution should produce.

The other approach is to assess institutional design based on specific properties of the institution (Olsen, 1997; 2007). Institutional design is seen as the appropriate way of coping with certain challenges. The aim is to secure that institutional practices and rules are consistent with basic principles and ideas in a polity. The legitimising principle of a certain design is linked to rules and practices that secure specific values such as the rule of law, impartiality, and neutrality (Olsen, 1997). Accordingly, institutions are not designed to secure a certain outcome, but rather designed to constrain processes in certain ways and allow for different substantive outcomes.

These two approaches involve different assessments of institutional design. Regarding the first, the legitimising principle of a certain design is connected to the substantive outcome of an institution. This would mean that special institutions ensure that future generations are considered in contemporary decision-making. While it is impossible to measure the future outcome, one can measure whether considering future people is decisive for today's decisions. In terms of the second, institutions are designed to encourage some types of behaviour and inhibit others. This would ensure that political norms are created to make decisions based on long-term thinking. This more flexible approach places more emphasis on norms than on measuring outcomes. Both approaches are crucial to analyse self-imposed collective binding constraints through institutions.

To understand what self-imposed constraints for future generations imply, it is helpful to discuss Boston's (2021) concept of political commitment devices. Commitment devices, Boston argues, "whatever their precise design or institutional form, seek to bind a person, organisation or government to an agreed course of action or particular norms or rules" (Boston, 2021, p. 87). In democracies, commitment devices are mechanisms to ensure that governments endorse and sustain measures to safeguard future-oriented goals. Commitment devices are institutional measures that help reduce long-term compliance problems. According to Boston, commitment devices are assumed to work by limiting future discretion or reinforcing self-restraints by increasing the cost of taking the easy way out. They can change the intertemporal payoff structure.

Boston's concept is broad. He presents a catalogue with 18 different types of political commitment devices. These are ranked from the global level with international goals to the use of policy nudging designed to alter the behaviour of citizens. Commitment devices can be hard or soft, formal, informal, public, private, procedural, substantive, unilateral, bilateral, imperative or reputational, and finally self-defined or externally defined. They can also be ranked along a continuum of bindingness (Boston, 2021).

There is a crucial difference between how Boston defines commitment devices and how institutional constraints are understood in this book. The four types of self-imposed institutional constraints analysed in this book are included in Boston's list of political commitments devices. Boston (2021) includes the whole policy cycle in his concept from policy initiation and agenda setting, policy formulation, decision-making, and implementation to evaluation and termination. In contrast, this book distinguishes between commitments in the form of statements and arguments reflecting ideas and motivations as the first dimension of solidarity, and the implementation of commitments in practice in the form of self-imposed institutional constraints as the second dimension.

How to show social solidarity with future generations

The second part of this book contains empirical analyses of four policy areas where normative commitments towards future generations are combined with some kinds of politically and legally binding actions. Chapter 5 analyses the UN's 2030 agenda, Chapter 6 investigates national institutions for future generations, Chapter 7 examines constitutions with clauses for future generations and climate lawsuits, and Chapter 8 analyses financial debt and savings for future generations. These four cases reveal how concerns for future generations are expressed both globally and nationally, and shows commitments encompassing political, legal, and economic policy issues and institutions.

The overarching question raised, as presented in Chapter 1, concerns when and how these commitments are followed up in practice, and what characterises situations where they are not followed up. Moreover, the question is raised as to whether and how there are differences between countries and policy areas and what we can learn from comparing them.

The analytical tool suggested for assessing these questions is a two-dimensional concept of solidarity with future generations. As discussed earlier, the first comprises ideas of indirect reciprocity with future generations, while the second concerns the willingness to establish self-imposed institutional bindings for the sake of future generations.

What is required to show social solidarity with future generations? How can we recognise it in empirical studies? To analyse these concrete questions, solidarity with future generations is operationalised by specifying three subquestions that will be analysed empirically.

1 What do the *commitments* to future generations involve?
2 How *binding* are the commitments for future generations when implemented in institutional practice?
3 What other societal concerns are in *tension* with the institutional bindings for the sake of future generations?

These three questions are adapted to and examined in each of the empirical studies in Chapters 5–8.

The first two questions are extracted from the two dimensions of solidarity. The first question refers to the first dimension of solidarity and thereby what kinds of ideas, attitudes, and motivations the commitments to future generations involve. The commitments are expected to include ideas of indirect reciprocity with future generations. These ideas are based on different understandings of temporality and narratives, which are brought together in a concept of framing (Entman, 1993). In the empirical studies, various frames and changes in frames over time can be found by analysing commitments expressed in laws, political agreements, and declarations.

The second question refers to the second dimension of solidarity regarding the current generations' willingness to establish self-imposed institutional constraint on current actions for the sake of future people. It concerns the extent to which commitments towards future generations are followed up in practice. This is examined by analyses of institutional amendments or the establishment of new institutions.

In combination, these two dimensions constitute the concept of solidarity with future generations. By examining empirically if and how there are combinations of commitments to future generations and institutional constraints we can say something about what it takes to show social solidarity with future generations.

Moreover, by elucidating the third question in each of the empirical chapters, we will be able to reveal which central aspects of society are at stake when we include the concern for future generations in today's political decisions and what tensions arise. This question pays attention to the country contexts in which the institutions exist (Hill, 2013), which this book describes as the *German dilemma* and the *Norwegian paradox*. The contextual factors also relate to the key political dynamics involving combinations of short-sighted mindsets or frames and societal structures discussed in Chapter 1 regarding democratic myopia.

Summary

- Studies of intergenerational justice are useful for understanding the complexities and uncertainties underlying concerns for future generations.
- Theories of intergenerational justice suggest abstract principles, which have limited function as analytical tools in empirical studies.
- Solidarity is suggested to be a more helpful concept to studying what is practically possible by the way it combines commitments with binding institutions.
- This chapter develops a two-dimensional concept of solidarity with future generations.
- The first dimension, justice as reciprocity, is reformulated to indirect reciprocity, which means giving something to a person, but it is not the same person who gives something in return.

- The second dimension, willingness, is reformulated to establish self-imposed institutional bindings to ensure that government endorses and sustains measures to safeguard future-oriented goals.
- The question of what is required to show social solidarity with future generations is operationalised by three sub-questions, which are analysed in Part II of this book: (i) What do the commitments to future generations involve? (ii) How binding are the commitments for future generations when implemented in institutional practice? (iii) What other societal concerns are in tension with the institutional bindings for the sake of future generations?

References

Anderson, B. (1991). *Imagined communities: Reflections on the origin and spread of nationalism*. Verso.

Bazzani, G. (2023). Climate solidarity: A framework and research agenda for low-carbon behaviour. *Sociological Forum*, *38*(2), 352–374.

Boston, J. (2021). Protecting long-term interests: The role of Institutions as commitment devices. In J. Linehan, & P. Lawrence (Eds.), *Giving future generations a voice: Normative frameworks, institutions and practice* (pp. 86–107). Edward Elgar.

Brown Weiss, E. (1992). In fairness to future generations and sustainable development. *American University International Law Review*, *8*(1), 19–26.

Caney, S. (2018). Justice and future generations. *Annual Review of Political Science*, *21*, 475–493.

Connelly, J., Smith, G., Benson, D., & Saunders, C. (2012). *Politics and the environment. From theory to practice*. Routledge.

Entman, R. M. (1993). Framing: Towards clarification of a fractured paradigm. *Journal of Communication*, *43*(4), 51–58.

Gómez-Franco, I. (2024). Amplified solidarity with future generations. *Philosophies*, *9*(17), 1–4.

Goodin, R. E. (1996). Institutions and their design. In R. E. Goodin (Ed.), *The theory of institutional design* (pp. 1–54). Cambridge University Press.

Gosseries, A. (2011). Three models of intergenerational reciprocity. In A. Gosseries, & L. H. Meyer (Eds.), *Intergenerational justice* (pp. 119–146). Oxford University Press.

Gosseries, A., & Meyer, L. H. (Eds.) (2011). *Intergenerational justice*. Oxford University Press.

Gough, I. (2017). *Heat, greed and human need. Climate change, capitalism and sustainable wellbeing*. Edward Elgar.

Habermas, J. (2015). *The lure of technocracy*. Polity Press.

Heath, J. (2013). The structure of intergenerational cooperation. *Philosophy & Public Affairs*, *41*(1), 31–66.

Hill, M. (2013). *The public policy process*. Pearson.

Kates, M. (2015). Justice, democracy, and future generations. *Critical Review of International Social and Political Philosophy*, *18*(5), 508–528.

Lawrence, P. (2014). *Justice for future generations: Climate change and international law*. Edward Elgar.

MacKenzie, K. (2021). *Future publics. Democracy, deliberation, and future-regarding collective action*. Oxford University Press.

Olsen, J. P. (1997). Institutional design in democratic contexts. *The Journal of Political Philosophy*, *5*(3), 2003–229.

Olsen, J. P. (2007). *Europe in search of political order. An institutional perspective on unity/diversity, citizens/their helpers, democratic design/horizontal drift, and the coexistence of orders*. Oxford University Press.
Parfit, D. (2017). Future people, the non-identity problem, and person-affecting principles. *Philosophy & Public Affairs*, *45*(2), 118–157.
Rawls, J. (1971). *A theory of justice*. Harvard University Press.
Rawls, J. (2001). *Justice as fairness. A restatement*. Harvard University Press.
Sen, A. (2009). *The idea of justice*. Harvard University Press.
Sen, A. (2013). The ends and means of sustainability. *Journal of Human Development and Capabilities*, *14*(1), 6–20.
Stjernø, S. (2005). *Solidarity in Europe: The history of an idea*. Cambridge University Press.
Stjernø, S. (2015). Solidarity beyond Europe? In J. Salamon (Ed.), *Solidarity beyond borders: Ethics in a globalising world* (pp. 1–27). Bloomsbury Publishing.
Thiery, W., Lange, S., Rogelj, J., Schleussner, C-F., Gudmundsson, L., Seneviratne, S.I., Andrijevic, M., Frieler, K., Emanuel, K., Geiger, T., Bresch, D.N., Zhao, F., Willner, S.N., Büchner, M., Volkholz, J., Bauer, N., Chang, J., Ciais, P., Dury, M., (…) & Wada, Y. (2021). Intergenerational inequities in exposure to climate extremes. Young generations are severely threatened by climate change. *Science*, *374*(6564), 158–160. https://www.science.org/doi/10.1126/science.abi7339
Thompson, J. (2011). Identity and obligation in a transgenerational polity. In A. Gosseries, & L. H. Meyer (Eds.), *Intergenerational justice* (pp. 25–49). Oxford University Press.
Tong, S., Samet, J. M., Steffen, W., Kinney, P. L., & Frumkin, H. (2023). Solidarity for the Anthropocene. *Environmental Research*, *235*, 116716.
Tremmel, J. (2009). *A theory of intergenerational justice*. Earthscan.
Tremmel, J. (2021). The four-branches model of government: Representing future generations. In M.-C. C. Segger, M. Szabo, & A. R. Harrington (Eds.), *Intergenerational justice in sustainable development treaty implementation. Advancing future generations rights through national institutions* (pp. 754–780). Cambridge University Press.
UN Secretary-General. (2013). Intergenerational solidarity and the needs of future generations. Report of the Secretary-General. United Nations General Assembly. Sixty-eighth session. 5 August. Retrieved 30.04.2024 from https://digitallibrary.un.org/record/756820?v=pdf
UN World Population Prospects. (2022). United Nations. World population prospects 2022: Summary of results. Retrieved 16.04.2024 from https://www.un.org/development/desa/pd/sites/www.un.org.development.desa.pd/files/undesa_pd_2022_wpp_key-messages.pdf
WCED. (1987). World Commission on environment and development. Our common future. Retrieved 24.04.2024 from http://www.un-documents.net/our-common-future.pdf

PART II

Solidarity in Practice

5

THE UN 2030 AGENDA AND FUTURE GENERATIONS

Introduction

In September 2015, all 193 UN member states signed *Transforming Our World: The 2030 Agenda for Sustainable Development*. With this agenda, the member states aimed to start a new global political process. The 2030 Agenda was presented as a charter for people and the planet in the twenty-first century, and it called for action to change our world. The agenda is universal as its 17 Sustainable Development Goals (SDGs) and 169 associated targets apply to all signatory countries. The global political process connected to the UN's 2030 Agenda expresses significant commitments to take future generations into consideration (UN 2030 Agenda, 2015).

This chapter analyses how the concern for future generations is presented in the global political process connected to the UN's 2030 Agenda. Three questions are formulated as an operationalisation of the concept of solidarity with future generations, as discussed in Chapter 4. (i) What do the commitments related to the 2030 Agenda to take future generations into consideration involve? (ii) How binding are the commitments in the 2030 Agenda for future generations when implemented in practice? (iii) What other societal concerns are in tension with the institutional constraints for the sake of future generations connected to the UN's 2030 Agenda?

The first section discusses global commitments to future generations in a broad context, while the second section traces the global political process associated with the 2030 Agenda from the Stockholm Declaration in 1972 through to 2014. The third section examines how the 2030 Agenda in 2015 includes concerns for future generations. The fourth section analyses the political process at the UN level that follows the 2030 Agenda from 2015 until

DOI: 10.4324/9781003400806-7
This chapter has been made available under a CC-BY-NC-ND 4.0 license.

the end of 2023. The fifth section discusses a series of calls for actions in the UN system, while the sixth section analyses the relationship between global commitments and national implementation.

The empirical investigations concentrate on UN documents linked to the UN's 2030 Agenda from 1972 until 2023, including UN Charters, General Assembly resolutions, declarations, and reports and policy briefs from the Secretary-General. The final section discusses theoretical proposals for global institutional constraints.

Social norms and global commitments to future generations

Global commitments to future generations date back to the Charter of the United Nations from 1945, in which the preamble begins with "We the peoples of the United Nations determined to save succeeding generations from the scourge of war, (…)" (UN Charter, 1945). Since then, a growing number of UN General Assembly resolutions, declarations, and Secretary-General reports and policy briefs have expressed concern for the welfare of future generations (UN Secretary-General, 2013; UN Our Common Agenda, 2021). These concerns cut across all issue areas as the obligations of present generations to future ones have been invoked more frequently and more urgently. In this context, the UN Secretary-General points out that at least 394 General Assembly resolutions explicitly mentioned "future generations" between 1961 and 2023 (UN Policy Brief, 2023). Together, these UN documents imply global obligations to safeguard the welfare of future generations. The UN is a crucial driving force in formulating the need to consider future generations.

The common heritage of mankind was introduced in international law in the 1960s. It established that certain global commons belong to all humanity, and their resources are available for everyone, also future generations (Taylor, 2011; 2017). This confirms that the concern for future generations is inherently part of the global commons (Brown Weiss, 2021).

Behind these global commitments to future generations, there is an underlying social norm stating that certain natural resources of the earth belong to everyone. These are physical resources such as the planet's natural environment, including the atmosphere, the ozone layer, the global system cycles, the climate system, as well as genetic and species diversity. These resources constitute the global commons, which can be understood as the world's common heritage that must be safeguarded for current and future generations (UNESCO, 1997). The global commons are, however, difficult to safeguard because they do not belong to any state and are not subject to state sovereignty, and all states and non-state actors can potentially exploit these resources (Riddervold & Akasemi, 2021).

Accordingly, a key international declaration on the issue was the UNESCO Declaration on the Responsibilities of the Present Generations Towards

Future Generations from 1997 (UNESCO, 1997). Of particular interest is Article 8: "The present generations may use the common heritage of humankind, as defined in international law, provided that this does not entail compromising it irreversibly" (UNESCO, 1997, Article 8).

The global commons represent a problem for collective action, and any attempt to utilise the resources can easily lead to what Harding (1968) called the "tragedy of the commons." This tragedy refers to situations where everyone has access to common resources, and the use of these is not regulated through common institutional arrangements. Certain actors can use these in a way that is contrary to the common interests of all users (Maxton & Randers, 2016). Uncoordinated actions can lead to the depletion of common resources, as Ostrom writes, "much of the world is dependent on resources that are subject to the possibility of a tragedy of the commons" (Ostrom, 1990, p. 3). However, Ostrom showed ways of collective use of limited collective resources. She had an institutional approach to public policy, and emphasised the creation of common institutions that bind the actors (Ostrom, 1990).

Regarding the global commons and the issue of creating global solutions at the UN level, the following three sections examine the political process from 1972 to 2023, as expressed in documents connected to the 2030 Agenda.

The process that led to the UN 2030 Agenda in 2015

Some UN Charters, General Assembly resolutions, declarations, reports, and policy briefs from the Secretary-General are of particular relevance for the political process leading to the 2030 Agenda. A concern for future generations linked to the natural environment emerged in the UN Conference on the Human Environment, which led to the Stockholm Declaration in 1972. This declaration stated we have reached a point in history when we must shape our actions throughout the world with more prudent care for their environmental consequences. Accordingly, the first principle says "Man…bears a solemn responsibility to protect and improve the environment for present and future generations" (UN Stockholm Declaration, 1972, Principle 1). This was followed up in the second principle.

> The natural resources of the earth, including the air, water, land, flora and fauna and especially representative samples of natural ecosystems, must be safeguarded for the benefit of present and future generations through careful planning or management, as appropriate.
>
> *(UN Stockholm Declaration, 1972, Principle 2)*

With this declaration the natural environment was framed as a global ecological common that needs to be safeguarded for all people today and in the future. A common language was created about nature as an ecological system with clear limitations, where consideration for our descendants is essential. This was in line with the knowledge of the field, such as the book *Limits to Growth* (Meadows et al., 1972).

This was followed up in the well-known understanding of sustainable development, defined by the World Commission on Environment and Development (WCED). As discussed in previous chapters, sustainable development was defined as development that meets the need of the present without compromising the ability of future generations to meet their own needs (WCED, 1987, Chapter 2, No. 1). The concern for future generations is inherent in this concept. The commission also appealed to the responsibility of current generations due to the future generations' lack of political and economic influence.

> We borrow environmental capital from future generations with no intention or prospect of repaying. They may damn us for our spendthrift ways, but they can never collect on our debt to them. We act as we do because we can get away with it: future generations do not vote; they have no political or financial power; they cannot challenge our decisions.
>
> *(WCED, 1987, Chapter 1, No. 25)*

Moreover, the Commission emphasised that social, economic, and ecological policies are closely connected and must be balanced against each other in a holistic approach at the global level. In political and academic debates following the commission, sustainability is often defined as a combination of social, economic, and ecological dimensions (Gough, 2017). Sustainable development is often a balancing act between conflicting social, economic, and ecological policies. While sustainable development is often exclusively linked to environmental threats, sustainable welfare is perceived in terms of the social and economic dimensions (Koch et al., 2016).

The way the WCED defined sustainable development has set the standard for how the concern for future generations is understood in later political and academic debates (Brown Weiss, 2021). Sustainability is connected to long-term thinking and opposes short-termism in meeting only the needs and interests of present generations. This definition has also functioned as a common guiding norm in several UN documents.

In Rio de Janeiro in 1992, the UN member states adopted UN Agenda 21. This agenda emphasised a "common concern" and encouraged governments to adopt a national strategy for sustainable development. Such strategies should protect the resource base and the environment for the benefit of future generations (UN Agenda 21, 1992). Moreover, Agenda 21 encouraged governments:

> To incorporate environmental costs in the decisions of producers and consumers, to reverse the tendency to treat the environment as a "free good"

and to pass these costs on to other parts of society, other countries, or to future generations.

(UN Agenda 21, 1992, Paragraph 8.31)

This was an appeal to nation states to handle the global commons as something that needs to be safeguarded for all people today and in the future. It can be interpreted as an argument for a collective orientation that touches on the tension between national actions and cosmopolitan ideals. This also implies an extension of the boundaries regarding whom one should act in solidarity with.

Similar types of arguments were used in 2000, when UN member states adopted the Millennium Declaration, which defined eight Millennium Development Goals (MDGs) to reduce extreme poverty by 2015. The objective with the MDGs was to establish common guiding norms for the development activities of the UN, for national priority-setting and for mobilisation of stakeholders and resources towards common goals. In common with Agenda 21, this declaration refers to how unsustainable patterns of production and consumption "must be changed in the interest of our future welfare and that of our descendants" (UN Millennium Declaration, 2000, p. 2). Once again, the boundaries of whom one should act in solidarity with was extended to future generations.

In 2012, in Rio de Janeiro, (Rio +20) UN member states endorsed the outcome document *The Future We Want*. This document is a comprehensive action plan to achieve sustainable development through cosmopolitan actions. It starts by presenting a common vision to renew the commitment to sustainable development and ensure "the promotion of an economically, socially and environmentally sustainable future for our planet and for present and future generations" (UN The Future We Want, 2012, Paragraph 1). Moreover, *The Future We Want* considered the need for promoting intergenerational solidarity to achieve sustainable development, recognising the needs of future generations, and it invited the Secretary-General to present a report on this issue.

In 2013, the UN Secretary-General published the report *Intergenerational Solidarity and the Needs of Future Generations* (UN Secretary-General, 2013). As mentioned in Chapter 4, this report discussed how intergenerational solidarity was embedded in the concept of sustainable development. It did not operate with a clear definition of solidarity. The UN report summarised how the consideration of future generations is included in many international treaties and agreements and how institutions for future generations have been created in some nation states in the world. The report presented possible models to institutionalise a concern for future generations at global and national levels.

The most important recommendation at the global level was to establish a UN High Commissioner for Future Generations as an international institution within the UN system. This would have a scope of action significantly different from national institutions that serve the needs of future generations (UN Secretary-General, 2013). Such a High Commissioner would be a way of institutionalising guiding norms for collective actions as also suggested in the scholarly literature (Aguis & Busuttil, 2013; Lawrence, 2021). This recommendation has not been implemented.

Ambitious UN 2030 Agenda in 2015

The UN 2030 Agenda begins by referring to how 70 years ago an earlier generation of world leaders came together to create the UN from the ashes of war. In comparison, the agenda from 2015 is presented as a charter for people and the planet in the twenty-first century, which involves all people from the international to the local level of civil society. The 2030 Agenda states:

> The future of humanity and of our planet is in our hands. It lies also in the hands of today's younger generation who will pass the torch to future generations. We have mapped the road to sustainable development; it will be for all of us to ensure that the journey is successful and its gains irreversible.
> *(UN 2030 Agenda, 2015, p. 12)*

These statements emphasise the concern for safeguarding the global commons of the currently living generations. There are no expectations of reciprocity, rather it is based on a perception of indirect reciprocity. In the 2030 Agenda, we can find references to future generations, including the future of humanity or of all people (UN 2030 Agenda, 2015). These references include both the objective to establish a good world for current and future people, and the use of the phrase future generations.

The three dimensions of sustainability are also inherent in the 2030 Agenda with the SDGs. The agenda includes themes ranging from poverty, health, education and inequality to energy, infrastructure, climate change, marine resources, peace, security, and good governance. Unlike its predecessor, the Millennium Goals, the SDGs are universal. Whereas the Millennium Goals concentrated on specific challenges faced by developing countries, the SDGs aim to solve common problems and secure economic, social, and environmental gains for everyone (UN 2030 Agenda, 2015). Above all, as Gough (2017) argues, the SDGs take the concern for future generations' social conditions seriously.

The 2030 Agenda also refers to the protection of the planet from degradation "so that it can support the needs of the present and future generations" (UN 2030 Agenda, 2015, p. 2). While the concern for future generations is defined and included as a global guiding norm, all references are limited to the preamble and declaration (UN 2030 Agenda, 2015).

The 17 SDGs are as follows:

1 No poverty
2 Zero hunger
3 Good health and well-being
4 Quality education
5 Gender equality
6 Clean water and sanitation
7 Affordable and clean energy
8 Decent work and economic growth
9 Industry, innovation, and infrastructure
10 Reduced inequalities
11 Sustainable cities and communities
12 Responsible consumption and production
13 Climate action
14 Life below water
15 Life on land
16 Peace, justice, and strong institutions
17 Partnerships for the goals

None of the 17 SDGs or 169 associated targets mentions future generations, and the temporal scope in the goals is weak (Oliveira, 2018). Although there may be an emergence of a broader normative consensus, the binding commitments to act in solidarity with future generations are thus rather weak.

Nevertheless, these stated commitments create some constraints. In these political processes where UN member states agree to consider future generations, they also create a common framing and language to discuss the challenges of dealing with long-term global policies (Coomans, 2023). In this respect, the political processes linked to the 2030 Agenda can be compared to how the human rights discourse has created a new language and a shared understanding. Accordingly, Lewis (2021) argues that human rights should provide the basis for institutions for future generations. Her argument is that human rights provide the language to articulate the rights and duties for future generations, and they provide a framework for decision-making. Human rights highlight the shared humanity between current and future generations and can thus put pressure on politicians to justify policies that take future generations into account. However, Lewis (2021) states that human rights are insufficient and there is a need for future-focused institutions that can incorporate the rights of future generations.

The common language linked to the 2030 Agenda and the SDGs has mainly developed from the increased capacity to generate knowledge about the future impacts of contemporary actions. Today's climate science has become more sophisticated, and scientific knowledge is made available to decision-makers through the Intergovernmental Panel on Climate Change (IPCC, 2024) reports. Similarly, scientific knowledge from the Intergovernmental Platform on Biodiversity and Ecosystem Services (IPBES, 2024) strengthens the role of science in public decision-making on biodiversity and ecosystem services. These panels spread the knowledge that the world's global resources are limited, and that today's generations must place limitations on themselves if our descendants are to be able to live dignified lives. With the 2030 Agenda, the concern for future generations has gradually been extended to include social and economic conditions as well.

This common language on the concern for future generations is linked to broader development, where this concern is included in several international treaties (Segger, 2021).

Together with the Paris Agreement on climate change, which was also signed in 2015, the 2030 Agenda aimed to shape a global action plan to solve problems that will have significant consequences for future generations. Both agreements are based on recognising the importance of acting now for future living conditions. Both have set clear goals to be achieved in 2030, and both agreements have institutions at the UN level with the task to monitor the extent to which the world has achieved the goals.

Despite the 2030 Agenda's calls to action to change our world, this is not intended to transform the traditional state system. The agenda confirms that every state has full sovereignty over its wealth, natural resources, and economic activity, and the 2030 Agenda is to be implemented in a manner that is consistent with the rights and obligations of states under international law (UN 2030 Agenda, 2015). The 2030 Agenda involves thereby a tension between common global commitments and sovereign states' willingness to implement these commitments in national policy.

Follow-up of the 2030 Agenda

In the process after the 2030 Agenda, there is an increasing demand for actions to follow up the commitments to future generations. Due to the agenda's statement about state sovereignty, the main challenges with these agreements are linked to how they are followed up by the nation states. Accordingly, Segger et al. (2021) argue that the concern for intergenerational equity included in international treaty law and sustainable development make a duty of the signatory states to implement their treaty obligations. The authors expect the states to take domestic action "for the protection and conservation of the elements of nature and the transmission of natural heritage to future generations" (Segger et al., 2021, p. 2). Moreover, they argue that global protection fails to deliver the desired result, and therefore, national institutions with the mandate to protect future generations may offer a complementary means of implementing commitments (Segger et al., 2021).

Even though the 2030 Agenda has a short time horizon (Oliveira, 2018), we may expect as Soltau (2021) does that by strengthening the norms in the agenda and encouraging governments to fulfil the SDGs, it will advance the interests of future generations. However, that presupposes the goals are met, and there is still a long way to go.

In 2012, the UN established the United Nations High-Level Political Forum on Sustainable Development (HLPF). The Forum is the central UN platform for the follow-up and review of the 2030 Agenda and the SDGs at the global level. It meets annually and every four years under the auspices of the General Assembly. The forum prepares annual reviews of progress towards the SDGs. These reviews are based on reports from the member states, which the member states produce voluntarily. The 2023 Voluntary National Reviews Synthesis Report is based on reports from 38 countries plus the European Union. The report includes numerous examples of

> (...) environmental devastation due to the worsening effects of climate change and accelerated biodiversity loss, including earthquakes, hurricanes, drought and disasters that in some countries will require many additional years of recovery. Ongoing and sustained conflicts continue to directly affect many countries, creating regional humanitarian crises, forcing the displacement and migration of millions of people, exacerbating extreme poverty and food insecurity, and rendering uncertain futures for a generation of children and youth.
>
> *(HLPF, 2023, p. 8)*

This type of self-reporting is similar to the requirement under the Paris Agreement that the parties submit their transparency report and national inventory report by 31 December 2024 at the latest (UN Climate Change, 2024). Such self-reporting aims to increase transparency in these global political processes.

Another annual report on the achievement of the SDGs is the UN's Sustainable Development Reports (Sachs et al., 2023). This is published by the Sustainable Development Solutions Network, which is a non-profit organisation created in 2012 by the United Nations to promote the SDGs at national and international levels. This report is based on data from a mix of official and non-official sources such as databanks of international organisations such as UNICEF, the World Health Organization, the World Bank, and peer-reviewed journals (Sachs et al., 2023). The 2023 Report is particularly interesting because it is the mid-term report. In the summary of key findings and recommendations, the UN Report concludes:

> At the midpoint of the 2030 Agenda, all of the SDGs are seriously off track. From 2015 to 2019, the world made some progress on the SDGs, although this was already vastly insufficient to achieve the goals. Since the

> outbreak of the pandemic in 2020 and other simultaneous crises, SDG progress has stalled globally.
>
> *(Sachs et al., 2023, p. vi)*

Furthermore, this UN report concludes that most high-income countries only make limited progress regarding the environmental and biological diversity goals. It refers to SDG 12 (Responsible consumption and production), SDG 13 (Climate action), SDG 14 (Life below water), and SDG 15 (Life on land). The report highlights that this applies to countries largely to blame for climate and biodiversity crises. According to the report, these crises have intensified financial challenges in low-income and lower-middle-income countries, which has led to a reversal in the progress of several goals. The UN report nevertheless concludes that the SDGs are still achievable and that none of the goals is beyond our reach. It writes "The world is off track, but that is all the more reason to double down on the SDGs" (Sachs et al., 2023, p. vi).

The most significant problem for countries in the global North is the transition from fossil fuels to renewable energy. In this context, the production of fossil energy is crucial. This will have significant consequences for future generations. The goals of the Paris Agreement and how the signatory countries have followed them up are also regularly monitored. The conflict is evident between the agreement on global commitments and national implementation. As mentioned in Chapter 1, the 2023 edition of the Production Gap Report reveals that the 20 major fossil-fuel-producing countries in the world plan to produce around 110% more fossil fuels in 2030 than would be consistent with limiting global warming to 1.5°C and 69% more than would be consistent with 2°C (UNEP, 2023). The report shows an ever-widening production gap for fossil fuels over time, which means a gap between plans for producing fossil fuels and what is consistent with limiting global warming to 1.5°C.

This mismatch between the global commitments to future generations inherent in the 2030 Agenda and the nation states' implementation in practice is well known. This knowledge has led to what Linehan and Lawrence (2021) describe as a "burgeoning scholarship" on institutions for the future. Researchers have therefore proposed to establish global institutions that treat intergenerational questions as a prioritised concern. Lawrence (2021) suggests, for example, maximising democratic legitimacy at the international level and discusses in a general way how this can be implemented with a High Commissioner. The aim is to make global institutions more responsive to the threat to the global ecosystems and the future people affected (Lawrence, 2021).

Another example is that Gardiner (2022) suggests a global constitutional convention focused on future generations which pay special attention to the global level and over the long term. Gardiner highlights six guidelines. These state the convention must have a mandate to consider a wide range of global cross-generational issues, be a permanent institution, have proxy representation, have an indefinite time horizon of at least centuries, be accountable to other institutions, and produce proposals adapted to the task. These guidelines are global and a holistic response to today's threats (Gardiner, 2022). Such suggestions are built on cosmopolitan solidarity, which emphasises supranational solutions that cross nation states' administrative and territorial organisation and encompass the entire world. Today, there are no such global institutions with a mandate to consider future institutions, but there are many ideas and proposals for how this can be done.

According to Caney (2022), there is a lack of overview of various proposals for supra-state institutions enacted to give protection to future generations. He has made such an overview by discussing contributions from different scholarly disciplines and has evaluated them in relation to the criteria effectiveness, legitimacy, distributive justice and liberty, and attainability. By evaluating ten different proposals he concludes that there is a considerable variation, but many proposals draw inspiration from existing global initiatives (Caney, 2022). Moreover, he argues that it is crucial to put the global arrangements in a context and emphasises the role of local, state, transnational, and global reforms to ensure that future people receive the protection to which they are entitled (Caney, 2022).

UN documents – call for actions

The mismatch between the global commitments inherent in the 2030 Agenda and the nation states' implementation in practice has led to the production of new UN documents calling for actions to follow up. In the political process that followed the 2030 Agenda from 2016 to 2023, four key documents are particularly relevant regarding the concern for future generations. Firstly, on the 75th anniversary of the UN, the member states agreed on a declaration in which they both affirmed the UN as a global organisation and simultaneously emphasised that the UN Charter is a cornerstone of international law based on states' sovereignty and respect for their territorial integrity (UN75 Declaration, 2020). This balancing act is the basis for all obligations member states agree they have towards the people of the future.

The declaration describes the 2030 Agenda as a roadmap, and its implementation as necessary for survival. The declaration confirms that the member states are determined to implement the 2030 Agenda fully and on time and that "There is no alternative" (UN75 Declaration, 2020, p. 2). Furthermore, it highlights the need to curb greenhouse gas emissions and achieve sustainable consumption and production patterns in line with the Paris Agreement and the 2030 Agenda: "This cannot wait" (UN75 Declaration, 2020, p. 2). These confirmations show an awareness of the need to act. "What we agree today, will affect the sustainability of our planet as well as the welfare of generations for decades to come" (UN75 Declaration, 2020, p. 4). Accordingly, the member states agreed to arrange a Summit of the Future in September 2024. The declaration pledged to strengthen global governance for current and future generations and requested the Secretary-General to make recommendations to respond to current and future challenges (UN75 Declaration, 2020).

Secondly, in 2021, the Secretary-General responded with the report *Our Common Agenda*. He called it a wake-up call to speed up the implementation of the SDGs and advance the commitments in the UN75 Declaration.

> Just as the founders of the United Nations came together determined to save succeeding generations from the scourge of war, we must now come together to save succeeding generations from war, climate change, pandemics, hunger, poverty, injustice and a host of risks that we may not yet foresee entirely. This is Our Common Agenda.
>
> *(UN Our Common Agenda, 2021, p. 18)*

While this agenda requires today's actions to encompass a broader range of challenges, including the viability of human life on earth, the report states we are far from keeping that promise (UN Our Common Agenda, 2021).

The report argues that the complex problems we face today, and our decisions, will influence the livelihoods of the 10.9 billion people expected to be born this century, predominantly in Africa and Asia. Moreover, it suggests that accounting for the interests of future generations would require adaptations. One is to build long-term thinking into important policies and decision-making, and the other is to create specific forums and instruments to protect future generations' interests at all governance levels. Both are specified in the policy brief published in 2023.

Thirdly, in 2022, a UN General Assembly resolution recognised the human right to a clean, healthy, and sustainable environment, and this includes commitments to future generations.

> Recognizing that sustainable development, in its three dimensions (social, economic and environmental), and the protection of the environment, including ecosystems, contribute to and promote human well-being and the full enjoyment of all human rights, for present and future generations.
>
> *(UN General Assembly, 2022, p. 2)*

Furthermore, the resolution recognises that environmental degradation, such as climate change and loss of biodiversity, poses some of the most severe threats to the ability of current and future generations to enjoy all human rights effectively (UN General Assembly, 2022).

Fourthly, in 2023, the Secretary-General published a policy brief *To Think and Act for Future Generations* (UN Policy Brief, 2023). This is the first in series of policy briefs to provide more detail on certain proposals contained in Our Common Agenda and prepared for the Summit of the Future in 2024. The policy brief emphasises that the current generations' obligations must act in a way that considers future generations and this "has already been enshrined in countless international agreements and in the very concept of sustainable development" (UN Policy Brief, 2023, p. 5). This refers to the 394 General Assembly Resolutions that have explicitly mentioned "future generations," as shown earlier. In addition, the policy brief has an Annex II that contains a partial list of 51 existing international instruments that refer to future generations such as charters, conventions, declarations, etc. However, the policy brief argues that these agreements are broken daily.

Proposals for UN institutions for future generations

This contradiction between repeated commitments and lack of follow-up in practice creates the basis for the policy brief's call for action. The purpose of this policy brief is therefore to present proposals for practical steps to fulfil the commitments. It proposes four specific steps "From commitment to reality" (UN Policy Brief, 2023, p. 15). Two steps are linked to the UN system and two steps are for the member states to agree on at international level.

One proposal linked to the UN system is to appoint a special Envoy to serve as a voice for future generations. The Envoy would perform advisory and advocacy functions for the interests of future generations across the UN system. The UN Policy Brief (2023) proposes several concrete functions. In general, these involve supporting member states and the UN system in raising awareness of intergenerational or future impacts of policies and proposing efforts to embed future generations and long-term thinking in global, national, and subnational policymaking. Moreover, the UN Policy Brief proposes that the Envoy would report annually to the General Assembly and/or a potentially dedicated intergovernmental forum.

The other suggestion linked to the UN system is to provide for better use of foresight, science, and data. The Policy Brief states that the capacity to generate knowledge about future impacts has improved in recent decades and refers to how the 2030 Agenda has led to efforts to use data and scientific knowledge more systematically. Some of the examples it refers to are the Data Strategy of the Secretary-General, the Futures Lab network, and the regular production of a global risks report (UN Policy Brief, 2023). However, the policy brief argues that more could be done to build a knowledge base on future impact. The intention is that an Envoy will have knowledge and be an advocate for the future, thereby ensuring that more sustainable decisions are made.

The two remaining steps proposed are for the member states to agree on. One suggestion is to adopt a declaration making the commitment to future generations concrete. The Policy Brief proposes how the declaration could define and make our duties to future generations concrete by listing 16 elements.

These include, among other things, recognising the importance of today's actions for future generations, and taking this into account in policymaking at all levels.

The other step for the member states to agree on is establishing a dedicated intergovernmental mechanism for debating and sharing best practices. The Policy Brief proposes the creation of a standing intergovernmental forum for future generations under the auspices of the General Assembly. While such a forum would not be a decision-making body, the UN Policy Brief (2023) states it could provide a locus for debate and collaboration.

As this type of institutions still does not exist at the UN level, and the Secretary-General's proposal from 2013 to establish a High Commissioner for Future Generations has never been followed up, these proposals are modelled after national political institutions. The Policy Brief argues that most of these national models have in common that they seek to understand the future impact of our choices today and communicate this understanding to decision-makers.

> It is these practices that we could now pursue at the international level to translate our long-standing global commitments into practical action, and to foster and support additional efforts at the national level in a broader range of countries.
>
> *(UN Policy Brief, 2023, p. 9)*

Altogether, these are proposals to reduce the mismatch between commitments to future generations in the 2030 Agenda and the absence of global institutions to monitor the implementation at the nation state level.

Global commitments and national implementation

By tracing the global process at the UN level that led to the 2030 Agenda, we have seen that the global commitments to secure future generations increased in scope and strength from 1972 to 2015. The commitments culminated in 2015 with the 2030 Agenda that was presented as a charter to change the world in the twenty-first century. This is an extremely ambitious programme, which is challenging to implement in practice.

Nevertheless, these commitments create a common language to categorise and describe the world's challenges and solutions. By agreeing to consider future generations, member states simultaneously establish common frames for discussing the challenges of managing long-term global policy. The SDGs provide a framework for decision-making. As we have seen, Entman (1993) emphasises that the common frames select some aspects and make them more salient. The frames promote a particular problem definition, causal interpretation, moral evaluation, and/or treatment recommendation.

With the 2030 Agenda, the common frames are established in the context of the increased capacity to generate knowledge about the future effects of modern actions. The knowledge that the world's global resources are limited is crucial to understanding that today's generations must set limits on themselves if our descendants are to live dignified lives. The frames regarding the concern for future generations is also linked to broader development, where this concern is included in several other international treaties (Segger, 2021).

Furthermore, the commitments in the 2030 Agenda create institutional constraints on the UN member states by how bodies within the UN system monitor the countries' achievement of the SDGs and publish the results in open global databases. This includes data from the countries' self-reporting evaluated by the UN High-Level Political Forum on Sustainable Development, and data from several independent sources evaluated and reported in the UN's Sustainable Development Reports. The main point is that each country's implementation of the SDGs is measured, and the results are published so everyone can see them.

The common frames and the monitoring of the member states' achievements are mechanisms that make the commitments morally binding, but they are still weak. As we have seen, midpoint reports reviewing the SDGs' achievements show that all SDGs are seriously off-track. The UN's institutions are weak because they have no authority over nation states' policies, and their tasks are limited to reporting and monitoring. The most essential form of sanction is shame, which has proven to be a meagre means of power in international politics.

The mismatch between the global commitments to future generations in the 2030 Agenda and the nation states' implementation in practice stems from tensions between global commitments and nation states' sovereignty. Nation states do not follow up on implementing what they have agreed on globally, and no global institution has the authority to lay pressure on countries to implement the 2030 Agenda and the SDGs.

There is thus a series of calls from the UN system for future-focused global institutions that can incorporate the concern for future generations. The number of calls has increased in recent years, and the proposals are presented as a step from commitment to reality. They build on previous discussions and proposals, such as the suggestion to appoint a special Envoy for future generations, and they have many of the same tasks as the proposal to establish a UN High Commissioner for Future Generations from 2013 (UN Policy Brief, 2023). The previous proposal was never realised in practice, but whether an Envoy will be established remains an open question.

None of these proposals from the UN Secretary-General involves a transfer of sovereignty to a global organisation. This means that the tensions between the sovereignty of nation states and global commitments to future generations are maintained. As various agreements are made piecemeal globally and are expected to be implemented in the nation states, it is challenging to implement global institutional bindings in practice.

Summary

- Global commitments to safeguard future generations have increased in scope and strength from 1972 and culminated with the ambitious goals of the UN 2030 Agenda.
- The commitments agreed on in the 2030 Agenda and the SDGs are creating a common frame to categorise and describe the world's challenges and solutions.
- Institutions within the UN system monitor countries' achievements of the SDGs and publish them in open global databases.
- The common frame and the monitoring of the member states' achievements are mechanisms that make the commitments morally binding.
- These bindings are weak, and the institutional constraints for future generations are only partly implemented in practice.
- There are tensions in the implementation of the SDGs between the sovereignty of nation states and global commitments to future generations.
- No global institution has the authority to put pressure on countries.
- Midpoint reports reviewing achievements show that all SDGs are seriously off-track.
- The mismatch between the global commitments to future generations in the 2030 Agenda and the nation states' implementation in practice has led to a series of calls for action in the UN system.

References

Aguis, E., & Busuttil, S. (Eds.) (2013). *Future generations and international law*. Routledge.

Brown Weiss, E. (2021). The theoretical framework for international legal principle of intergenerational equity and implementation through national institutions. In M.-C. C. Segger, M. Szabo, & A. R. Harrington (Eds.), *Intergenerational justice in sustainable development treaty implementation. advancing future generations rights through national institutions* (pp. 16–43). Cambridge University Press.

Caney, S. (2022). Global climate governance, short-termism, and the vulnerability of future generations. *Ethics and International Affairs*, *36*(2), 137–155.

Coomans, F. (2023). Towards 2122 and beyond: Developing the human rights of future generations. *Netherlands Quarterly of Human Rights*, *41*(1), 53–60.

Entman, R. M. (1993). Framing: Towards clarification of a fractured paradigm. *Journal of Communication*, *43*(4), 51–58.

Gardiner, S. (2022). On the scope of institutions for future generations: Defending an expansive global constitutional convention that protects against squandering generations. *Ethics and International Affairs*, *36*(2), 157–178.

Gough, I. (2017). *Heat, greed and human need. Climate change, capitalism and sustainable wellbeing*. Edward Elgar.

Harding, G. (1968). The tragedy of the commons. *Science*, *162*, 1243–1248.
HLPF. (2023). High-level political forum. 2023 Voluntary national reviews synthesis report. Retrieved 25.01.2024 from https://hlpf.un.org/sites/default/files/2023-12/2023_VNR_Synthesis_Report.pdf
IPBES. (2024). Intergovernmental platform on biodiversity and ecosystem services document search. Retrieved 02.05.2024 from https://www.ipbes.net/documents
IPCC. (2024). Intergovernmental panel on climate change. Documentation. Retrieved 02.05.2024 from https://www.ipcc.ch/documentation/
Koch, M., Gullberg, A. T., Schoyen, M. A., & Hvinden, B. (2016). Sustainable welfare in the EU: Promoting synergies between climate and social policies. *Critical Social Policy*, *36*(4), 704–715.
Lawrence, P. (2021). International institutions for future generations and democratic legitimacy. In M.-C. C. Segger, M. Szabo, & A. R. Harrington (Eds.), *Intergenerational justice in sustainable development treaty implementation. Advancing future generations rights through national institutions* (pp. 597–613). Cambridge University Press.
Lewis, B. (2021). Human rights as a basis for institutions for future generations. In J. Linehan, & P. Lawrence (Eds.), *Giving future generations a voice. normative frameworks, institutions and practice* (pp. 62–84). Edward Elgar.
Linehan, J., & Lawrence, P. (Eds.) (2021). *Giving future generations a voice. Normative frameworks, institutions and practice*. Edward Elgar.
Maxton, G., & Randers, J. (2016). *Reinventing prosperity*. Greystone Books.
Meadows. D. H., Meadows, D. L., Randers, J., & Behrens W. W. (1972). *The limits to growth*. Universe Books.
Oliveira, R. V. (2018). Back to the future: The potential of intergenerational justice for the achievement of the sustainable development goals. *Sustainability*, *10*, 427. http://doi.org/10.3390/su10020427
Ostrom, E. (1990). *Governing the commons. The evolution of institutions for collective actions*. Cambridge University Press.
Riddervold, M., & Akasemi, N. (2021). Introduction: Cooperation, conflict, and interaction in the global commons. *International Relations*, *35*(3), 365–383.
Sachs, J. D., Lafortune, G., Fuller, G., & Drumm, E. (2023). *Implementing the SDG stimulus. Sustainable development report 2023*. Dublin University Press. Retrieved 06.03.2024 from https://dashboards.sdgindex.org/
Segger, M.-C. C. (2021). International treaty law and policy for future generations. In M.-C. C. Segger, M. Szabo, & A. R. Harrington (Eds.), *Intergenerational justice in sustainable development treaty implementation. Advancing future generations rights through national institutions* (pp. 47–67). Cambridge University Press.
Segger, M.-C. C., Szabo, M., & Harrington, A. R. (Eds.) (2021). *Intergenerational justice in sustainable development treaty implementation. Advancing future generations' rights through national institutions*. Cambridge University Press.
Soltau, F. (2021). The 2030 Agenda for sustainable development: What are its implications for future generations? In J. Linehan, & P. Lawrence (Eds.), *Giving future generations a voice. Normative frameworks, institutions and practice* (pp. 108–126). Edward Elgar.
Taylor, P. (2011). Common heritage of mankind principle. In K. Bosselmann, D. Fogel, & J. B. Ruhl (Eds.), *The encyclopedia of sustainability: The law and politics of sustainability* (pp. 64–69). Berkshire Publishing.
Taylor, P. (2017). Governing the global commons: An ethical-legal framework. *Policy Quarterly*, *13*(1), 43–49.
UN 2030 Agenda. (2015). Transforming our world: The 2030 Agenda for sustainable development. Resolution adopted by the General Assembly on 25 September 2015. Retrieved 24.04.2024 from https://documents.un.org/doc/undoc/gen/n15/291/89/pdf/n1529189.pdf?token=pi8KVlOSHwSRbar7mV&fe=true

UN Agenda 21. (1992). United Nations conference on environment & development Rio de Janeiro, Brazil, 3 to 14 June 1992. Agenda 21, paragraph 8.7. Retrieved 03.05.2024 from https://sustainabledevelopment.un.org/content/documents/Agenda21.pdf

UN Charter. (1945). Charter of the United Nations. Retrieved 18.01.2024 from https://untso.unmissions.org/sites/default/files/united_nations_charter.pdf

UN Climate Change. (2024). Preparing for the enhanced transparency framework. Retrieved 16.04.2024 from https://unfccc.int/process-and-meetings/transparency-and-reporting/preparing-for-the-ETF

UN75 Declaration. (2020). *Declaration on the commemoration of the seventy-fifth anniversary of the united nations—A/RES/75/1*. https://www.un.org/pga/74/wp-content/uploads/sites/99/2020/07/UN75-FINAL-DRAFT-DECLARATION.pdf

UNEP. (2023). SEI, Climate Analytics, E3G, IISD, and UNEP. Phasing Down or Phasing Up? Top Fossil Fuel Producers Plan Even More Extraction Despite Climate Promises: Production Gap Report 2023. https://doi.org/10.51414/sei2023.050

UNESCO. (1997). Declaration on the responsibilities of the present generations towards future generations. Retrieved 17.01.2024 from https://www.unesco.org/en/legal-affairs/declaration-responsibilities-present-generations-towards-future-generations

UN General Assembly. (2022). Promotion and protection of human rights: Human rights questions, including alternative approaches for improving the effective enjoyment of human rights and fundamental freedoms. Resolution 76/300. Retrieved 18.01.2024 from https://documents-dds-ny.un.org/doc/UNDOC/GEN/N22/442/77/PDF/N2244277.pdf?OpenElement

UN Millennium Declaration. (2000). Resolution adopted by the General Assembly on 18 September 2000. Retrieved 03.05.2024 from https://www.un.org/en/development/desa/population/migration/generalassembly/docs/globalcompact/A_RES_55_2.pdf

UN Our Common Agenda. (2021). Report of the Secretary-General. Retrieved 17.01.2024 from https://www.un.org/en/content/common-agenda-report/assets/pdf/Common_Agenda_Report_English.pdf

UN Policy Brief. (2023). To think and act for future generations. Retrieved 17.01.2024 from https://www.un.org/sites/un2.un.org/files/our-common-agenda-policy-brief-future-generations-en.pdf

UN Secretary-General. (2013). Intergenerational solidarity and the needs of future generations. Report of the Secretary-General. United Nations General Assembly. Sixty-eighth session. 5 August. Retrieved 30.04.2024 from https://digitallibrary.un.org/record/756820?v=pdf

UN Stockholm Declaration. (1972). Declaration of the United Nations conference on the human environment. Retrieved 03.05.2024 from https://wedocs.unep.org/bitstream/handle/20.500.11822/29567/ELGP1StockD.pdf

UN The Future We Want. (2012). Resolution adopted by the General Assembly on 27 July 2012, paragraph 1. Retrieved 03.05.2024 https://sustainabledevelopment.un.org/content/documents/733FutureWeWant.pdf

WCED. (1987). World Commission on Environment and Development. Our common future. Retrieved 24.04.2024 from http://www.un-documents.net/our-common-future.pdf

6
NATIONAL POLITICAL INSTITUTIONS FOR FUTURE GENERATIONS

Introduction

With the UN 2030 Agenda, the world's countries developed a common language around several issues and committed themselves to including future generations in current policies. However, these commitments have not led to an agreement to establish global institutions for future generations. It is thereby up to the individual countries to establish their own national political institutions for future generations. Two types of national political institutions have the potential to implement the commitments for future generations. One type ensures the country's implementation of the 2030 Agenda with the Sustainable Development Goals (SDGs). The other type has a specific mission for future generations and aims to ensure they are represented in current policy. Both are established to secure a long-term policy and often overlap in practice.

This chapter analyses if and how these two types of political institutions for future generations can compensate for politicians' modest ability to lay down guidelines for long-term solutions. Three questions are formulated as an operationalisation of the concept of solidarity with future generations, as discussed in Chapter 4. (i) What do the *commitments* by establishing national political institutions for future generations involve? (ii) How influential are the political institutions in ensuring that commitments for future generations are *binding* in practice? (iii) What other societal concerns are in *tension* with the political institutions' constraints on current policies for the sake of future generations?

These questions are answered by studying existing political institutions for future generations. Firstly, the chapter provides a general review of various

DOI: 10.4324/9781003400806-8
This chapter has been made available under a CC-BY-NC-ND 4.0 license.

types of institutions based on documents from the UN and the International Energy Agency. This overview also includes public documents from Canada, Finland, and Hungary as examples of countries with such institutions. Secondly, the chapter discusses how Germany has institutionalised the implementation of the SDGs and how these institutions take future generations' concerns into account. The German documents are from across several government departments and the *Bundestag* (parliament). Thirdly, the chapter conducts similar analysis of Norwegian institutions. The Norwegian documents are from across several government departments and the *Storting* (parliament). The document study also includes the German and Norwegian voluntary national reviews to the UN High-Level Political Forum (HLPF). Fourthly, the chapter presents and discusses various suggestions for institutional constraints, and fifthly, it concludes that the institutions have weak political influence on contemporary policies.

Different types of political institutions

In Rio de Janeiro in 1992, the UN member states adopted UN Agenda 21, which encouraged governments to adopt national Sustainable Development Strategies (UN Agenda 21, 1992). The aim was to translate ideas and commitments of the Rio Conference into concrete policies and actions. Subsequently, the plan of implementation agreed on in Johannesburg in 2002 recommended governments to formulate "national strategies for sustainable development and begin their implementation by 2005" (UN Report Johannesburg, 2002, p. 71). Moreover, it aimed:

> To further promote the establishment or enhancement of sustainable development councils and/or coordination structures at the national level including at the local level, in order to provide a high-level focus on sustainable development policies.
>
> *(UN Report Johannesburg, 2002, p. 72)*

An underlying social norm for promoting the establishment of such institution is that future generations should be politically represented. Political representation means the activity of making citizens' voices, opinions and perspectives present in the public policymaking process, and there are many forms of representation, such as formal, substantial, symbolic, and descriptive (Pitkin, 1967). In the case of unborn people, this is proxy representation, meaning someone is appointed to defend future generations' assumed challenges and interests. This norm about the need for proxy representation is linked to "democratic myopia," the tendency of short-sightedness in both mindset and structures of democratic decision-making processes (MacKenzie, 2021; Smith, 2021). These mindsets and structures imply that future generations are excluded from contemporary political decisions that are important to their lives, and they have no economic or political power to influence decisions.

Consequently, the absence of political representation of future generations means that conflicts of interest between generations are decided by a majority of eligible voters, not the majority of those affected by the decision (Tremmel, 2021). The main reason is the time lag between political decisions and their consequences. As such, we can often observe that politicians and the institutional arrangements do not consider future generations in elections or political decisions (Vermassen et al., 2023). Against this background, researchers point out that contemporary democracies were developed in the nineteenth century and are not designed for today's challenges, where the most significant consequences of today's decisions will come in the future (Smith, 2021; Tremmel, 2015).

The political representation of future generations can take several forms. Democratic procedures can, for example, promote intergenerational justice by proxy representations by giving extra votes to persons representing future generations because they cannot represent themselves (Caney, 2018; Kates, 2015). The decisive question is how influential the political institutions are in ensuring that measures for future generations are binding in practice.

The UN Secretary-General's Report from 2013 is a good starting point for analysing how this encouragement to establish national political institutions for future generations is followed up (UN Secretary-General, 2013). As shown in Chapter 5, this UN report discussed how intergenerational concern is embedded in the concept of sustainable development. It presented models to institutionalise concern for future generations at the global and national levels. At the global level, the UN report suggested a High Commissioner for Future Generations, which has not been established. At the national level, the UN Report reviews how Canada, Finland, Hungary, Israel, New Zealand, and Wales (United Kingdom of Great Britain and Northern Ireland) either have or have had an office that serves to protect the needs of future generations. In line with this category of countries, the UN Report also highlights one institution in Germany: German Parliamentary Advisory Council on Sustainable Development, and one in Norway: Norwegian Ombudsperson for Children (UN Secretary-General, 2013).

Several scholars have followed up this UN report. Their aim has been to discuss the already functioning national political institutions for future generations (Brown Weiss, 2021; Dirth & Kormann da Silva, 2022; Krajnyak, 2023; Mathis et al., 2022; Segger et al., 2021; Smith, 2021; Tremmel, 2021). Many scholars highlight the existing institutions as models and emphasise the importance of learning from these institutions (e.g. Szabo, 2021). Most of these studies do not clearly distinguish between institutions that will ensure the countries' implementation of sustainable development and those that are specifically designed for future generations. As Krajnyak (2023) argues, only some of the eight institutions mentioned in the UN Report from 2013 directly advocate for future generations. They defend the environment, sustainable development, and children. These themes are indirectly linked to care for future generations and future-oriented policies.

These discussions show that in the political and academic debate, a distinction is made between two types of institutions that can impact whether and how future people are included in contemporary politics. Several countries worldwide have established political institutions to ensure the country's implementation of their sustainable development strategies. After the agreement on the 2030 Agenda in 2015, these institutions were tasked with ensuring that the countries follow up on the SDGs. Mathis et al. define sustainable institutions as "public, trans-departmental and permanent national bodies with an integrated understanding of sustainability that considers socioecological well-being, global context and future orientation" (Mathis et al., 2022, p. 1). This type of institution offers a broad institutional framework for policy that extends beyond day-to-day decisions and provides for longer-term policy. These institutions do not particularly focus on future generations, but the countries implementing the SDGs indirectly consider this. There is no record of how many of these there are in the world. Such institutions have a wide range of tasks and must constantly balance them with short-term needs.

Dirth and Kormann da Silva (2022) believe that institutions with a mandate for future generations make greater use of the opportunity to focus on long-term dynamics. They concentrate on institutions designed to have a specific mission for future generations and count 16 countries with such institutions in the world: Australia, Canada, Finland, Germany, Gibraltar, Goa (India), Hungary, Israel, Malta, the Netherlands, New Zealand, Scotland, Singapore, Wales, United Kingdom, and Uruguay (although this counts Scotland, Wales, and the UK as separate entities). Dirth and Kormann da Silva (2022) counted twice as many institutions as reviewed in the UN Report from 2013. The study includes all the institutions included in the UN report, apart from the Norwegian one, as we return to in the following. This type of institution aims to provide future generations with proxy representation. These institutions are not exclusively linked to the SDGs but function within their framework.

While these two types of institutions have different mandates at the outset, they often overlap in practice because both aim to secure a long-term policy. Therefore, the following empirical analysis will treat them interchangeably, but it will clarify which type is being discussed. By establishing such institutions, countries have committed themselves to including the consideration of future people in current politics.

Institutions and proxy representation

As a backdrop for the analyses of German and Norwegian institutions, it is useful to gain an insight into various examples of institutions for future generations and how previous researchers have assessed them. According to their location in the political system, institutions for future generations can be divided into three main categories: institutions linked to parliament, institutions connected to government apparatus, and public institutions that are more or less independent.

Firstly, a concern for our descendants can be fostered by institutionalising representation for future generations in the parliament (Jones et al., 2018; Kates, 2015). One example is the Committee for the Future established in *Eduskunta*, the Finnish parliament, in 1993. This was the first permanent parliamentary committee with the task to have long-term considerations across all policy areas (Smith, 2021). The Committee is one of the *Eduskunta's* 16 standing committees, and it has 17 members based on a cross-party composition. The Committee's main functions are to scrutinise the Government's Report on the Future, which covers a wide range of topics related to, among other things, climate change, demographic change, and technological development (Finnish parliament, 2023). It also issues statements to other committees on matters related to the future. Since 2017, the Government's plan for the implementation of Agenda 2030 for Sustainable Development has also been submitted to the Committee (Finnish parliament, 2023). According to Tiihonen (2021), the Committee's main task is to think about various alternative futures, discuss them, and work for the best possible future for the people. The committee has neither legislative nor budgetary power, Tiihonen (2021) notes, but it can present initiatives and visions.

Secondly, political institutions designed for future generations can be government bodies, committees, and groups established within government apparatus. One example is the Canadian Commissioner of the Environment and Sustainable Development established in 1995. This Commissioner is embedded within the Office of the Auditor General which has the task of improving government accountability by auditing and reporting on the government's operations. The Commissioner has the task of providing analysis and recommendations on the federal government's efforts to protect the environment, mitigate the effects of climate change, and foster sustainable development (Auditor General of Canada, 2023). The Commissioner mainly issues reports on assessing whether departments of the Federal Government are meeting their sustainable development objectives. Future generations are not explicitly defined in the work of the Commissioner, but as Wright and McKenzie (2021) argue, an audit function can draw attention to and raise awareness of topics important to future generations.

Thirdly, political institutions designed to promote and defend the interests of future generations can be established outside the ordinary parliament and government institutions (Tremmel, 2021). Such independent institutions can be commissions, councils, or offices for future generations or ombudspersons who are appointed to investigate complaints against an institution and seek resolutions to those complaints. The main intention with such independent institutions is to bring in the long-term implications of actions and present alternatives essential for future generations' well-being from outside the ordinary political institutions (Smith, 2021).

One example is the Office of the Parliamentary Commissioner for Future Generations established in Hungary in 2007. It was terminated in 2011, and the institutional protection of future generations was transferred to the Commissioner for Fundamental Rights as one of two Deputies of the Commissioner (Commissioner for Fundamental Rights of Hungary, 2023). The deputy is called the *Deputy Commissioner for Future Generations* and functions as an ombudsman. Its main task is to monitor the enforcement of the interest of future generations. While the power of the previous commissioner was broader, Krajnyak (2023) argues that the power of the new commissioner is significant as it has an impact on key constitutional court decisions and can contribute to legislation-making by issuing legislative proposals. Also, Szabo (2021) argues that the Commissioner is a crucial pillar of the Hungarian legal system. Still, based on the evidence of the past decade, he concludes that while there are no constitutional constraints on the ombudsman's action, he or she cannot counterbalance other institutions of the Hungarian legal system (Szabo, 2021).

Such national political institutions for future generations have the potential to ensure proxy representation for our immediate descendants and people who have not yet been born. While some institutions have this as an explicitly formulated goal, others can indirectly provide for it. Through such institutional constraints, today's generations commit to a form of indirect reciprocity with the people of the future. However, in general, studies of these institutions show that they address the problems of political presentism, but they have a weak influence on ensuring that measures for future generations are binding in practice (Knebel, 2023; Krajnyak, 2023; Szabo, 2021; Tiihonen, 2021; Wright & McKenzie, 2021).

Institutions in Germany

Germany established its first national sustainable development strategy in 2002, and since then the strategy has been revised every fourth year. With the plan for the implementation of the 2030 Agenda in 2016, the SDGs were perceived as a follow-up of the German sustainable strategy, but the original catalogue of goals, subgoals and indicators was significantly altered

(Tremmel, 2014). In 2021, the federal government published a revised strategy, which stated that Germany follows the guiding principle of sustainable development "(...) meeting the needs of today's and future generations – in Germany and in all parts of the world – and allowing them fulfilled lives of dignity" (German Sustainable Development Strategy, 2021, p. 12).

The coordinating lead department for implementing the SDGs is the Federal Chancellery. Germany has established a State Secretaries' Committee which in practice serves as the central coordinator and ensures that the guiding principle of sustainable development is applied to all policy areas (German Review to the HLPF, 2021). This committee reports on its activities annually to the Federal Cabinet (German Sustainable Development Strategy, 2021). Hence, the governance of the sustainability strategy does not follow traditional ministerial hierarchies but is organised cross-sectorally.

Germany has established two institutions that attend the regular State Secretary Committee meetings and produce position papers. One is the Parliamentary Advisory Council on Sustainable Development, *Parlamentarischer Beirat für nachhaltige Entwicklung* (PBnE), as discussed in the following. The other is the German Council for Sustainable Development, *Rat für Nachhaltige Entwicklung* (RNE) established in 2000. The RNE has 15 members, who are individuals from civil society, the business sector, the scientific community, and the political arena. They are appointed by the Chancellor for a (renewable) term of three years. The RNE's task is twofold. One is to advise the government on its sustainable development policy, and the other is to foster public dialogue on the issue of sustainability. The RNE operates as an independent entity, and it has an office comprising 24 persons who carry out the day-to-day work (RNE, 2024).

The State Secretaries' Committee, the Parliamentary Advisory Council, and the Council for Sustainable Development show that Germany has established institutions in all three political arenas: in parliament, in government, and as an independent council. They are connected in the State Secretary Committee meetings. However, they have weak political influence (Bachmann, 2021). The institutions serve mainly as a reminder of how contemporary decisions will have significant consequences for the future. They do not have a special mandate to provide for future generations, but this can be achieved indirectly as far as Germany implements the SDGs.

In addition, Germany has institutions that are particularly relevant for climate and environmental issues, and two important institutions should be mentioned. One is the German Advisory Council on Global Change, *Wissenschaftlicher Beirat der Bundesregierung Globale Umweltveränderungen* (WBGU). In the period from 2020 to 2024, the advisory council consists of nine members appointed by the German government's Federal Cabinet for a four-year term. The members have special knowledge and experience of the Advisory Board's tasks. The WBGU is independent in its work and is monitored and supported by State Secretary Committee. The office has a secretariat consisting of 12 employees. They contribute with scientific expertise, coordinate processes, organise logistical workflows, and curate events (WBGU, 2024).

The other is the German Advisory Council on the Environment, *Sachverstandigenrat für Umweltfragen* (SRU). The seven members of the SRU are appointed for four years by the Federal Ministry for the Environment, Nature Conservation, Building and Nuclear Safety after approval by the Federal Cabinet. It comprises experts from various disciplines with special scientific knowledge and experience in environmental issues. Further selection criteria are "excellence, representativeness, professional networking, breadth of expertise and advisory orientation." The office has a secretariat consisting of 12 scientific employees (Tremmel, 2018).

A study of the German implementation of the SDGs found that Germany has come further than most European countries in thinking about, and to some extent institutionalising, a coordinated and holistic approach to sustainability (Schoyen et al., 2022). The German political conditions for developing a policy that combines the social, economic, and ecological dimensions of sustainable development should be rather good at the outset. Germany has a welfare state that builds on the historical tradition from Bismarck's social insurance reforms, and the country has been a forerunner of energy transition. With the *Energiewende* Germany has made efforts to replace power production relying on nuclear and fossil energy sources with renewable ones (Leiren & Reimer, 2018).

However, Germany has major barriers to the simultaneous priority of social, economic, and ecological goals. These are seen as conflicting goals, and politicians, trade unions, employers' organisations, and voluntary organisations prioritise them differently (Schoyen et al., 2022). Significantly, in terms of concrete results, Germany is struggling to meet the climate targets it has committed itself to at European and international levels.

This is evident in the country's profile in the annual published UN's Sustainable Development Report (Sachs et al., 2023). As discussed in Chapter 5, this report is based on data from a mix of official and other sources such as databanks of international organisations and peer-reviewed journals. The main point in using this is that it is based on independent evaluations and not self-reporting like the voluntary national reports to the HLPF, as discussed earlier. In the 2023 report, Germany is in fourth place of the 193 UN member states, behind Finland, Sweden, and Denmark. The countries that top the list are all rich welfare states in northern Europe, with three Scandinavian countries which have low population densities at the top. The UN report has developed a ranking regarding how each country has achieved the SDGs which goes from top scores, medium challenges, and significant challenges to major challenges. Based on this ranking system, the report shows that Germany has not achieved top scores on any of the SDGs. The country has medium challenges on ten SDGs, significant challenges on five goals and major challenges in achieving two goals.

The major challenges are in achieving the SDGs number 12 and 13. Number 12 is responsible consumption and production, and the problems are electronic waste, nitrogen emissions embodied in imports, and exports of plastic waste. The other is number 13, which is climate action. Germany has high CO_2 emissions from fossil-fuel combustion and cement production, and from emissions embodied in imports (Sachs et al., 2023). As a typical highly developed and affluent country Germany's ecological footprint far exceeds the planetary carrying capacity.

There is still a long way to go. According to the IEA World Energy Balances latest updated numbers from 2022, 78% of German energy consumption came from fossil sources, while 19% came from renewable energy. The same year nuclear power counted 3%, but its nuclear power stations were closed in 2023. From fossil sources, coal counted 20%, natural gas 24%, and oil 33%. Regarding renewable energy, hydro power counted 1%, wind and solar energy 6%, and biofuels 12% (IEA World Energy Balances, 2024a). According to the country's future development of greenhouse gas emissions, the progress is far from sufficient to reach the reduction targets for 2030.

Germany has not established an institution with a special mandate to represent future generations. The government has established a triangle of institutions to ensure the implementation of the SDGs, and in addition there are institutions that are particularly relevant for climate and environmental issues. The establishment of these institutions involves commitments to future generations. However, these institutions have weak influence on whether the long-term policy becomes binding in practice. They have not been mandated to intervene in political decisions but instead have a role as reminders that today's political decisions can have significant consequences in the future. They thereby contribute to and maintain a common language about the importance of long-term thinking and acting. This common frame of reference is crucial for current decision-making, but it is far from enough as is also confirmed with the German major challenges regarding the environmental SDGs.

Parliamentary Advisory Council in Germany

The UN Secretary-General's Report (2013) referred to the German Parliamentary Advisory Council on Sustainable Development, *Parlamentarischer Beirat für nachhaltige Entwicklung* (PBnE), as an example of an institution intended to serve as the advocate of long-term responsibility in the German political process. The PBnE was established in 2004, against a background of discussions about how the federal government's sustainability policy could be supported by the German *Bundestag* (Bundestag, 2022). The council has a central position in the German implementation of the SDGs by attending the regular State Secretary Committee meetings. It has a broad scope on sustainable development, and its activities will, therefore, indirectly include the concern for future generations. According to the council's homepage in the *Bundestag* its guiding principle behind policymaking is geared towards sustainability, "making sure that life today is not at the expense of tomorrow!" Moreover, the council presents itself as a "watchdog," which "barks" when an initiative fails to consider the National Sustainability Strategy (PBnE German Bundestag, 2024). According to a study carried out by Kinski and Whiteside (2023), the members of the council see themselves as representatives of future generations.

The PBnE is appointed by the *Bundestag* every electoral period. In the current period from 2021 to 2025, it has 20 members from all political parties proportionate to the parties' size in the *Bundestag*. In contrast to the standing committees in the *Bundestag*, which are directly assigned to a ministry, the council is interdisciplinary and cross-sectoral. Its mandate is to work with long-term tasks that go beyond day-to-day political disputes (PBnE German Bundestag, 2024). The council is assigned tasks when appointed, and each council thus has new tasks. There is therefore no reliable long-term basis for the council's work (Reimer, 2021).

The council's work programme for the 20th election period from 2021 to 2025 emphasises that sustainability is understood as an "ethical principle" (Bundestag, 2022). This principle, it states, requires a holistic view of social challenges, implying that the people living today are responsible to future generations. Furthermore, it argues that sustainability is not limited to environmental and nature conservation responsibility but also includes economics and social conditions. The current PBnE provides parliamentary support for the government's sustainability policy at the European and UN levels. This includes activities and measures to implement the SDGs in the 2030 Agenda. The *Bundestag* has also given the current council the task to submit proposals to the *Bundestag* on how the council's work can be made more efficient and communicate more effectively to the public (Bundestag, 2022). An important goal for the PBnE, the work programme states, is to be independent of changing majority ratios in the *Bundestag* and that it can thereby devote itself to its task with continuity across party lines (PBnE German Bundestag, 2024). From these documents we can read that decisions are expected to be cross-political and based on consensus.

One of the council's core tasks is to evaluate draft laws and regulations from the federal government. These evaluations take the form of hearings, briefings, motions for resolutions, statements, and position papers. The reference points for these evaluations are the indicators and goals of the German sustainability strategy. In the 19th legislative period from 2017 to 2021, the council evaluated 512 federal government projects with a view to assessing whether they had taken sustainable development into account (PBnE German Bundestag, 2021). The PBnE found that in 96% of cases, the federal government had considered sustainability and concluded that sustainability is an essential foundation for legislation (PBnE German Bundestag, 2021).

However, when the council checks whether the federal government has considered the draft laws' compliance with the prevailing sustainability principles, it does not make any qualitative assessments or judgements about whether the proposal meets the sustainability standards (Schoyen et al., 2022). A more substantive qualitative assessment would be time-consuming and difficult to obtain (Reimer, 2021). It could lead to more controversies and challenge how the council has operated according to a consensus principle. As Kinski and Whiteside (2023) argue, this consensus orientation seems appropriate for matters affecting future generations. The required consensus can be an obstacle to gaining traction for a future-oriented policy, which implies a weak representation of future generations. Moreover, the opinion of the council could be ignored as it has neither procedural nor substantive rights or competences towards the *Bundestag* and the committees (Bachmann, 2021; Reimer, 2021).

The explicitly formulated rationale for setting up the PBnE is to ensure that Germany designs an innovative, forward-looking policy (Bundestag, 2022). This means that its primary role is to maintain a common frame for moral evaluations and remind people of the importance of long-term policies. Studies of the council and debates in the *Bundestag* show that the council has raised awareness of the need for a forward-looking policy (Kinski & Whiteside, 2023). This is important for commitments to the future but not enough to secure institutional constraints that bind political decisions to long-term goals.

Lack of institutions in Norway

Like Germany, Norway adopted its first Sustainable Development Strategy in 2002. Since 2008, the implementation of this strategy has been included in the national budget process as part of the government's annual policy cycle. From 2016, the government implemented the SDGs as a follow-up of this strategy, and from 2016 to 2019 the Ministry of Finance coordinated the implementation. In 2020, this coordinating role at the domestic level was transferred to the Ministry of Local Government and Modernisation, while the Ministry of Foreign Affairs is responsible for contact with the UN and international bodies. This is an example of how government departments are often working in silos (Schoyen & Takle, 2022). The same year, a State Secretaries' committee for the SDGs was established, in which all ministries are represented (Norway's Review to HLPF, 2021). This is similar to the committee in Germany.

At the domestic level, the main responsibility for each of the SDGs lies with a single department. This means that the responsibility for the SDGs is divided between ministries and included in the daily political process. A challenge with this implementation is that the overall assessment and connection between the goals can be lost. This challenge is reinforced by the fact that Norway does not have an independent body responsible for implementing SDGs based on an overall assessment like the German Parliamentary Advisory Council and the Council for Sustainable Development. In Norway, this task is assigned to the Ministry of Local Government and Modernisation (Norway's Review to HLPF, 2021). This does, however, not create the same transparency around the processes as in Germany.

When the coordinating role for the domestic implementation of the SDGs was transferred to the Ministry of Local Government and Modernisation, it was simultaneously signalled that the SDGs should be anchored locally. Local anchoring is a central principle for the implementation of the SDGs at the UN level, and considerable effort to achieve the goals is made at the local level in Norway (Meld. St. 40, 2020–2021). This local focus can, however, mask the fact that Norway's major challenges in achieving the SDGs are linked to fundamental features of the Norwegian economy as discussed in Chapter 1 and require major efforts at the national level.

A study of Norway's implementation of the SDGs found that the country has struggled with a fundamental paradox for several decades, and there is still no convincing solution (Schoyen & Takle, 2022). Norway is well placed to achieve a coordinated implementation of the social, economic, and ecologic dimensions of sustainability.

> Norway is a small and very wealthy country, characterized by strong public finances, a coordinated market economy, a digitally advanced and efficient bureaucracy, and a comprehensive welfare state. People and businesses are accustomed to a state that makes active use of instruments such as taxes, economic incentives, and regulations to steer behaviour. These factors have contributed to relatively low levels of social inequality and high levels of trust in government.
>
> *(Schoyen & Takle, 2022, p. 153)*

Current and future prosperity can only be upheld as long as the economy relies on a highly profitable but carbon-intensive oil and gas sector. The country's comprehensive welfare state is supported by enormous revenues from carbon-intensive oil and gas extraction and exports. There is still a politically mainstream frame "that Norway can carry on with its oil and gas production, including the exploration and development of new fields, and nonetheless fulfil the commitments of the Paris Climate Agreement" (Schoyen & Takle, 2022, p. 170). This leads to obstacles for implementing the SDGs concerning the environment in Norwegian politics.

Sachs et al. (2023) confirm this pattern. In the 2023 UN Sustainable Development Report, Norway is in seventh place out of the 193 UN member states, behind its Scandinavian neighbours, Germany, Austria, and France (Sachs et al., 2023). Based on the report's ranking system from top scores, medium challenges, and significant challenges to major challenges regarding how each country has achieved the SDGs, the Norwegian scores differ slightly from the German scores. Norway has top scores on five SDGs, which are related to welfare state arrangements. Norway has medium challenges on six SDGs and significant challenges on two goals.

Norway has major challenges on four SDGs. There are major challenges concerning goal number two which emphasises zero hunger, and this is due to the indicators of obesity, too little plant food in the diet, and too much nitrogen fertiliser. There are major challenges regarding goal number 12, referring to responsible consumption and production. Norway has poor waste management and excessive emissions of sulphur dioxide (SO_2) and nitrogen through the import of consumer goods. There are major challenges regarding goal number 13, which is climate action. Norway has high CO_2 emissions generated through oil and gas exports, from fossil energy in transport and cement production, and generated through the import of consumer goods. Finally, Norway has major challenges regarding fulfilling goal number 15, which is life on land. The country protects small areas and freshwater areas in its own country (Sachs et al., 2023). Like Germany, and many other countries, Norway's ecological footprint far exceeds the planetary carrying capacity.

These results confirm that Norway has impressive results in terms of social and economic progress, but the country has a highly problematic position regarding the ecological dimension. To achieve its challenging SDGs, Norway tends to support initiatives outside the country, as discussed in terms of the Norwegian paradox (UN General Assembly, 2020). The Norwegian position has relied heavily on international emission trading. In simple terms, Norway offsets domestic emissions by paying for cuts in other countries to reach its climate targets (Boasson & Lahn, 2017). The reason is not only that the country's economy relies on oil and gas production.

According to the IEA World Energy Balances latest updated numbers from 2022, Norway has a special energy mix. About 50% of Norwegian energy consumption came from fossil sources, while about 50% came from renewable energy. From fossil sources, coal counted 3%, natural gas 22%, and oil 25%. Regarding renewable energy, hydro power counted 38%, wind and solar energy 5%, and biofuels 7% (IEA World Energy Balances, 2024b). The fact that Norway's renewable sources cover a high share of domestic energy consumption makes it relatively costly to cut emissions at home. This is another important reason why Norway offsets domestic emissions by paying for cuts in other countries to reach its climate targets.

Regarding the achievement of the SDGs, Norway can be said to be a leader abroad and a laggard at home (Schoyen & Takle, 2022). There is no indication that the 2021 Voluntary National Review and the new Norwegian national action plan – taken together – will be capable of bringing about a turning point in the domestic implementation process (Norway's Review to HLPF, 2021; Meld. St. 40 (2020–2021)).

This is reinforced by the fact that Norway has not established an independent institution responsible for implementing the SDGs based on an overall assessment, as Germany has. This lack of independent institutions creates less transparency around the implementation of the commitments in the SDGs. In Norway, the coordinating task has been assigned to the Ministry of Local Government and Modernisation and the implementation of the SDGs is linked to the municipal level. The political challenges and tensions involved in implementing the environmental SDGs depend on national political decisions. Regarding the high CO_2 emissions generated through oil and gas exports, there is a lack of a long-term policy that considers both today's young people and those who will be born in the future. This results in weak institutional bindings for future generations.

Ombudsperson for children in Norway

The UN Secretary-General's Report (2013) included the Ombudsperson for Children in Norway in the review of countries with institutions for future generations. This makes it interesting to take a closer look at how the ombudsperson serves this task. The Ombudsperson for Children was appointed in 1981, as the first in the world. It is designed to promote and defend the interests of children independent of government institutions. In contrast to the German Parliamentary Advisory Council on Sustainable Development, the Ombudsperson for Children has no place in the landscape of institutions with a special responsibility for implementing the SDGs.

According to the Ombudsperson's website, it has three duties. Firstly, to ensure that children and young people's opinions are heard, and their rights are upheld. Secondly, to ensure that the authorities in Norway comply with the Convention on the Rights of the Child, which is enshrined in Norwegian law. Thirdly, the ombudsperson is an independent body, forming its own opinions and deciding what areas to focus on (Ombudsperson for Children in Norway, 2023). Furthermore, the ombudsperson describes its way of influencing the authorities as holding lectures and seminars, writing letters to the authorities, and making statements when laws are written or amended. The ombudsperson also ensures contact with the media and participates in meetings with ministers and members of parliament (Ombudsperson for Children in Norway, 2023).

Neither this self-presentation nor the ways it works suggest that the ombudsperson is an institution for future generations. This is confirmed by an internet search on "future generations" on the ombudsperson's website.

It results in only four hits. While three hits concern the strengthening of children's participation in the work on climate challenges, one is related to children's upbringing conditions (Ombudsperson for Children in Norway, 2023).

There are not any reasons to believe that the Ombudsperson for Children is an institution designed to have a specific assignment for future generations. How can we understand that the UN Secretary-General's Report (2013) included this Ombudsperson in the review of countries with institutions for future generations? The answer to this question might be seen in the following statement.

> The welfare of future generations is in a large part determined by our treatment of children of current generations, which means that caring for future generations should have a special focus on investing in the human rights and development of the children of today. Concern for children in the context of intergenerational justice has surfaced in international human rights instruments, notably the Convention on the Rights of the Child.
>
> *(UN Secretary-General, 2013, p. 13)*

This statement suggests that consideration for future generations' welfare should focus on investing in the development of today's children. This is also the point of departure for a study conducted by Fauchald and Gording Stang (2021). By analysing the Ombudsperson's Act and the instructions for the ombudsperson, they contend that it is within the ombudsperson's mandate to promote the interest of future generations (Fauchald & Gording Stang, 2021). They argue that the ombudsperson has a duty to act in situations where environmental, social, and economic conditions are deteriorating so that children will suffer. The two authors believe this duty has been strengthened by the ratification of the Convention on the Rights of the Child in 1991 and incorporating it into Norwegian law in 2003, and by the inclusion of environmental protection for the sake of future generations in the constitution in 1992 and the constitutional reform in 2014, as returned to in Chapter 7.

However, by analysing the practice of the ombudsperson from 1981 to 2020, Fauchald and Gording Stang (2021) conclude it has only to a limited extent promoted the interest of future generations. Such promotion has been implicit, and occurred as a side effect of efforts to safeguard the interests of current generations. Moreover, the ombudsperson has primarily addressed economic and social conditions for future generations, while environmental conditions are rarely affected (Fauchald & Gording Stang, 2021). This priority is surprising in light of the youth's preoccupation with environmental changes. In 2022, the ombudsperson stated that climate and environment should be a priority area from that year. This was the year after the study by

Fauchald and Gording Stang (2021) was published. How the ombudsperson has implemented this is unclear, as this priority is not followed up in the annual report from 2022 (Ombudsperson for Children in Norway, 2023).

Fauchald and Gording Stang (2021) have a very good point in their call for the ombudsperson to act more actively concerning future generations.

> So far, public authorities, courts, parliamentary control mechanisms, and the Parliament itself have paid very limited attention to such provisions when proposing and adopting legislation, budgets, and policies. There is significant need for independent review of how these provisions are implemented in the interest of future generations. The Ombudsman for Children should see the constitutional reforms as an opportunity to strengthen its contribution to the living conditions of future generations of children.
> *(Fauchald & Gording Stang, 2021, p. 373)*

There is significant room for action for the Ombudsperson to strengthen and make more explicit contributions to the welfare of future unborn generations. This room for action is also reinforced by the lack of an independent body responsible for implementing the SDGs in Norway. This is particularly problematic given the political tensions involved in implementing the SDGs' environmental goals. Norway not only lacks institutions to ensure the implementation of binding long-term commitments towards future generations, but also has no national political institutions whose task is to raise awareness of the welfare of future generations.

Suggestions for institutional constraints

As discussed in Chapter 5, current political and academic debates about global and national institutions for future generations are mainly reminders of the future consequences of current decisions. Existing institutions are discussed as models to provide for long-term policies, and there are calls for actions to establish new institutions (Linehan & Lawrence, 2021, p. 11). While national institutions have the potential to ensure proxy representation for future generations, they are few and have only weak influence on if and how measures for future generations are binding in practice.

Due to the weaknesses regarding the links between commitments and binding institutional constraints in practice, theoretical proposals for how to design national institutional constraints for future generations have been instigated. As we shall see, academic literature suggests institutions within parliament, the government, and as independent bodies.

One proposal is to emphasise the principle of deliberation to encourage contemporary actors to consider and represent the interests of future generations. MacKenzie (2021) builds on a deliberative theory to discuss future-oriented collective action. He argues that we need inclusive, deliberative, democratic processes to create our common future collectively and mutually accommodatingly. Moreover, he states that the future should not only be predicted, but also be shaped or created through our collective future-making capacities. MacKenzie argues that deliberative practices such as reason giving, justification, and persuasion are needed to help coordinate the actions of the past, present, and future.

Regarding institutional design, he suggests that future-oriented democratic institutions will need to be "inclusive, deliberative and capable of acting independently from short term electoral dynamics and market imperatives" (MacKenzie, 2021, p. 25). Moreover, he emphasises that institutions must be able to deal with different types of temporally complex issues and the interdependencies between them. With these ideas as criteria, he assesses several different institutional arrangements. According to MacKenzie, deliberation can help encourage contemporary actors to consider and represent the interests of future generations. "Deliberation is the only institutional mechanism that I am aware of that may plausibly play this role in public affairs" (MacKenzie, 2021, p. 89).

Another proposal is to present a list of principles of institutional design that must be met to consider the long term and to safeguard the interests of future generations. Smith (2021) extracts five principles that underlie how we can promote long-term solutions and secure the interests of future generations. The first principle is to create independent institutions that are not subject to the pressure that, among others, elected politicians are exposed to. The second principle is diversity, which involves including the voices of all types of groups in democratic decisions, especially future generations. The third principle is deliberation, where Smith, like MacKenzie, emphasises the importance of justifying choices in public. The fourth principle is institutionalisation, where Smith argues, that compliance with political decisions over time requires permanent bodies that promote long-term thinking. The fifth principle is empowerment. Smith highlights that institutions created to defend the interests of future generations must have decision-making power. They must at least have the opportunity to veto or postpone decisions that do not consider the consequences the decisions will have for people who have not yet been born (Smith, 2021).

A third proposal is to establish a fourth branch in addition to legislative, executive, and judicial power. Tremmel (2021) suggests a future branch as a general model that can be adapted to different countries' historical traditions, as there is no single model that suits all countries. According to Tremmel (2021), this future branch might be called an ombudsperson, guardian, commissioner, committee, or something else. As a starting point, Tremmel sets up three conditions for the institution. It must have power, be able to intervene in legislative procedures, and be at the national level.

His model is three dimensional. The first dimension is agency. Tremmel emphasises that a fourth branch must have the opportunity to start a legislative process but not stop it by right to veto. The rationale is that a fourth branch should not be accused of representing an eco-dictatorship or a new veto player that could increase the possibilities of gridlock. The second dimension is the policy fields the branch should consider. While these might be all fields, environmental policy is seen as the most important. The third dimension is the composition of the members of the branch, and this is the diagonal dimension which crosses the first two dimensions. Tremmel suggests that the members should not be elected, but rather appointed by politicians, and a collective body is better shielded from criticism than one single person. Tremmel's (2021) main point is to launch a model for a fourth branch responsible for long-term thinking on behalf of future generations. The proposal is designed to be adapted to today's democracies and simultaneously change them so that the new institution is perceived as democratically legitimate.

Like MacKenzie and Smith, Tremmel's point of departure is that the current democracies require future-beneficial institutions. He draws on the history of ideas and refers to how one during the establishment of the democracies in the eighteenth century considered the system of checks and balances to protect minorities against the "tyranny of the majority." He compares this with how we today need an institutional design against the "tyranny of the present over the future" (Tremmel, 2021).

These authors highlight different principles in solving the problem of short-sightedness and thereby complement one another. The background for all three is that democracies fail to solve the challenges of the future, and they refer to democratic myopia or the tendency towards short-term thinking in democracies. Moreover, the scholars argue against the idea that to solve long-term problems we need other types of political systems that are less democratic or even authoritarian. In contrast, they emphasise that democracies need to be better adapted to the current situation in which decisions in the present can influence future people far more than in former times. As we have seen in these three theoretical suggestions, all authors emphasise the importance of formal institutional constraints to safeguard that future generations are considered.

Weak institutional bindings

National political institutions that consider long-term policies important for future generations can be of two types. One type ensures a country's implementation of the broad spectrum of SDGs, while the other has a specific mission for future generations. These two types of political institutions often overlap in practice as both are concerned with long-term policy as opposed to democratic myopia.

By establishing such institutions, countries commit themselves to implementing long-term policy important for future generations. Today's generations thereby commit to a form of indirect reciprocity with the people of the future. As we have seen, institutions for future generations can be institutions linked to the parliament or the government apparatus, and state institutions that are more or less independent. Many scholars who have studied such institutions conclude that the institutions have the potential to ensure proxy representation for future generations by addressing the problems of political presentism. Still, they conclude the institutions have a weak influence on ensuring that measures for future generations are binding in practice.

This analysis of the German and Norwegian cases shows similar patterns. Neither of the two countries has an institution with a special mandate to represent future generations. Both countries' measures to implement the SDGs are ways of ensuring a long-term policy that can impact future people.

Germany has more institutions than Norway. The country has a triangle of institutions provided with the tasks to ensure the implementation of the SDGs in parliament, in government, and as an independent state institution. These institutions involve commitments to future generations, but they act in an indirect way by participating in the implementing of the SDGs. As we have seen, they have a weak influence on making the long-term policy binding in practice.

One example is the German Parliamentary Advisory Council on Sustainable Development, which has not been mandated to intervene in political decisions and has no competences in relation to the *Bundestag*. The council has the mandate to check if the federal government has considered whether the draft laws comply with the sustainability principles, but it does not make any qualitative assessments. A more substantive qualitative assessment could lead to tensions and challenge the council's legitimacy, which is based on a consensus principle.

The council needs to achieve political consensus to gain political influence. This can be necessary to ensure legitimacy and stability in the support of long-term policy, but it can also be an obstacle for a future-oriented policy, leading to a weak representation of future generations. The council's role is to remind politicians of the importance of long-term policies. It can ensure that this is framed in a way that calls attention to future consequences of current decisions. This strengthens the commitments to the future, but it is not enough to establish institutional constraints that bind political decisions to long-term goals. Nevertheless, Germany has established far more institutions for future generations than Norway has done.

Norway has established neither political institutions with a special mandate to represent unborn future generations nor institutions to ensure the implementation of the SDGs. The Ombudsperson for Children in Norway is often mentioned in reviews of countries with institutions for future generations (UN Secretary-General, 2013). Neither the ombudsperson's self-presentation nor the ways it works suggests that it is an institution for people who have not yet been born. It is an institution for children and young people living today.

The implementation of the SDGs is assigned to the Ministry of Local Government and Modernisation and linked to the local level. This leads to less transparency in the implementation of the SDGs in Norway than in Germany. Moreover, the tensions involved in implementing the environmental SDGs cannot be solved at the local level. They are dependent on national political decisions influenced by the Norwegian paradox.

Both in Germany and Norway, there are tensions between the production and use of energy from fossil fuels and the consideration of long-term environmental challenges. The weak institutions for future generations can be linked to these political tensions.

Summary

- There are two types of national political institutions for future generations, which often overlap in practice because both consider long-term policies.
- While one type of political institution ensures a country's implementation of the broad spectrum of SDGs, the other type has a specific mission for future generations.
- By establishing such institutions, countries commit themselves to long-term policies important for future generations, but the institutions have weak political influence in ensuring that measures for future generations are binding in practice.
- Germany has established a triangle of the State Secretaries' Committee, the Parliamentary Advisory Council, and the Council for Sustainable Development.
- This triangle has a weak political influence on German politics, but serves as an important reminder of the importance of today's decisions for future people.
- The German Parliamentary Advisory Council operates on the basis of consensus and depends on the absence of significant political tensions to gain political influence, which means a weak representation of future generations.
- Norway does not have an independent institution responsible for implementing the SDGs based on an overall assessment. This task is assigned to the Ministry of Local Government and Modernisation and does not create the same transparency as in Germany.
- The Ombudsperson for Children in Norway only promotes the welfare of children and young people living today and cannot be said to provide proxy representation for people who have not yet been born.

- Weak institutions for future generations can be linked to political tensions, and in Germany and Norway, there are tensions between the production and use of energy from fossil fuels and consideration of long-term environmental challenges.
- Political institutions for future generations take shape as reminders of the future consequences of today's decisions and have a function in maintaining a common frame of commitments to future people.

References

Auditor General of Canada. (2023). The commissioner of the environment and sustainable development. Retrieved 20.12.2023 from https://www.oag-bvg.gc.ca/internet/English/au_fs_e_370.html#Commissioner

Bachmann, G. (2021). Transformative knowledge and solutions in sustainable governance. In M.-C. C. Segger, M. Szabo, & A. R. Harrington (Eds.), *Intergenerational justice in sustainable development treaty implementation. Advancing future generations rights through national institutions* (pp. 315–328). Cambridge University Press.

Boasson, E. L., & Lahn, B. (2017). Norway: A dissonant cognitive leader? In R. Wurzel, J. Connely, & D. Liefferink (Eds.), *The European Union in international climate change politics: Still taking a lead?* (pp. 189–203). Routledge.

Brown Weiss, E. (2021). The theoretical framework for international legal principle of intergenerational equity and implementation through national institutions. In M.-C. C. Segger, M. Szabo, & A. R. Harrington (Eds.), *Intergenerational justice in sustainable development treaty implementation. Advancing future generations rights through national institutions* (pp. 16–43). Cambridge University Press.

Bundestag, German. (2022). Establishment of the parliamentary advisory council for sustainable development for the 20th electoral period. *Drucksache*, 20/696. Retrieved 03.01.2024 from https://dserver.bundestag.de/btd/20/006/2000696.pdf

Caney, S. (2018). Justice and future generations. *Annual Review of Political Science*, *21*, 475–493.

Commissioner for Fundamental Rights of Hungary. (2023). The office of the commissioner for fundamental rights of Hungary. Retrieved 20.12.2023 from https://www.ajbh.hu/web/ajbh-en/about-the-office

Dirth, E., & Kormann da Silva, N. (2022). *Building our common future: The role of the network of institutions for future generations in safeguarding the future.* ZOE Institute for Future-fit Economies. Retrieved 06.05.2024 from https://zoe-institut.de/wp-content/uploads/2023/10/Building_Our_Common_Future_ZOE_Report_2022.pdf

Fauchald, O. K., & Gording Stang, E. (2021). Norway: Norwegian ombudsman for children. In M.-C. C. Segger, M. Szabo, & A. R. Harrington (Eds.), *Intergenerational justice in sustainable development treaty implementation. Advancing future generations rights through national institutions* (pp. 352–373). Cambridge University Press.

Finnish parliament. (2023). Committee for the future. Retrieved 20.12.2023 from https://www.eduskunta.fi/EN/valiokunnat/tulevaisuusvaliokunta/Pages/default.aspx?TSPD_101_R0=08d2c9383aab2000aa815c7cced879fcfe7ab2a9688e6dbe23dd5c76a84a52ca8eb4fc7734c5b0ca08389507ef143000c3af53e98ab8be8d3d3fd108161476429f5d55e94304ea4df16e1d8b00e90f968805afa8fff09c6d7ddccc5baad6169a

German Review to the HLPF. (2021). German voluntary national review to the UN high-level political forum on sustainable development. Retrieved 03.01.2024 from https://hlpf.un.org/sites/default/files/vnrs/2021/279522021_VNR_Report_Germany.pdf

German Sustainable Development Strategy. (2021). Retrieved 04.01.2024 from https://www.bundesregierung.de/resource/blob/974430/1940716/8943e3f421a7a0d8bcd06a1cc66e92d0/2021-07-26-gsds-en-data.pdf?download=1

IEA World Energy Balances. (2024a). International Energy Agency. World energy balances. Germany. Retrieved 09.01.2024 from https://www.iea.org/countries/germany

IEA World Energy Balances. (2024b). International Energy Agency. World energy balances. Norway. Retrieved 09.01.2024 from https://www.iea.org/countries/norway

Jones, N., O'Brien, M., & Ryan, T. (2018). Representation of future generations in United Kingdom policy-making. *Futures*, *102*, 153–163.

Kates, M. (2015). Justice, democracy, and future generations. *Critical Review of International Social and Political Philosophy*, *18*(5), 508–528.

Kinski, l, & Whiteside, K. (2023). Of parliament and presentism: Electoral representation and future generations in Germany. *Environmental Politics*, *32*(1), 21–42.

Knebel, M. (2023). Cross-country comparative analysis and case study of institutions for future generations. *Futures*, *151*, 103181, 1–14.

Krajnyak, E. (2023). The role and activity of the deputy commissioner for fundamental rights ombudsman for future generations in shaping environmental protection in Hungary. *Journal of Agricultural and Environmental Law*, *XVIII*(34), 7–30.

Leiren, M. D., & Reimer, I. (2018). Historical institutionalist perspective on the shift from feed-in tariffs towards auctioning in German renewable energy policy. *Energy Research & Social Science*, *43*, 33–40.

Linehan, J., & Lawrence, P. (Eds.) (2021). *Giving future generations a voice: Normative frameworks, institutions and practice*. Edward Elgar.

MacKenzie, K. (2021). *future publics. Democracy, deliberation, and future-regarding collective action*. Oxford University Press.

Mathis, O. L., Rose, M., Newig, J., & Bauer, S. (2022). Towards the sustainability state? Conceptualising national sustainability institutions and their impact on policy making. *Environmental Policy and Governance*, *33*(1), 1–12.

Meld. St. 40 (2020–2021). Goals with meaning — Norway's action plan to achieve the sustainability goals by 2030 (white paper). Retrieved 05.01.2024 from https://www.regjeringen.no/contentassets/bcbcac3469db4bb9913661ee39e58d6d/no/pdfs/stm202020210040000dddpdfs.pdf

Norway's Review to HLPF. (2021). Voluntary National Review Norway to the UN high-level political forum on sustainable development. Retrieved 03.01.2024 from https://www.regjeringen.no/contentassets/cca592d5137845ff92874e9a78bdadea/no/pdfs/voluntary-national-review-2021.pdf

Ombudsperson for Children in Norway. (2023). About the ombudsperson for children. Retrieved 20.12.2023 from https://www.barneombudet.no/english/

PBnE German Bundestag. (2021). Report of the parliamentary advisory council for sustainable development (Work report 19th legislative period). Drucksache 19/30130. Retrieved 03.01.2024 from https://dserver.bundestag.de/btd/19/301/1930130.pdf

PBnE German Bundestag. (2024). Parliamentary advisory council on sustainable development. Role and responsibilities. Retrieved 02.01.2024 from https://www.bundestag.de/en/committees/bodies/sustainability

Pitkin, H. F. (1967). *The concept of representation*. University of California Press.

Reimer, F. (2021). Institutions for a sustainable future: The German parliamentary advisory council on sustainable development. In M.-C. C. Segger, M. Szabo, & A. R. Harrington (Eds.), *Intergenerational justice in sustainable development treaty implementation. Advancing future generations rights through national institutions* (pp. 374–394). Cambridge University Press.

RNE. (2024). Rat für Nachhaltige Entwicklung. German Council for Sustainable Development. Retrieved 25.04.2024 from https://www.nachhaltigkeitsrat.de/en/

Sachs, J. D., Lafortune, G., Fuller, G., & Drumm, E. (2023). *Implementing the SDG stimulus. Sustainable development report 2023*. Dublin University Press. Retrieved 06.03.2024 from https://dashboards.sdgindex.org/

Schoyen, M. A., Koch, M., & Takle, M. (2022). Partially institutionalized eco-social policymaking in Germany. In M. A. Schoyen, B. Hvinden, & M. D. Leiren (Eds.), *Towards sustainable welfare states in Europe. Social policy and climate change* (pp. 109–130). Edward Elgar Publishing.

Schoyen, M. A., & Takle, M. (2022). The Norwegian sustainability paradox: Leader abroad, laggard at home. In M. A. Schoyen, B. Hvinden, & M. D. Leiren (Eds.), *Towards sustainable welfare states in Europe. Social policy and climate change* (pp. 153–174). Edward Elgar Publishing.

Segger, M.-C. C., Szabo, M., & Harrington, A. R. (Eds.) (2021). *Intergenerational justice in sustainable development treaty implementation. Advancing future generations' rights through national institutions*. Cambridge University Press.

Smith, G. (2021). *Can democracy safeguard the future?* Polity Press.

Szabo, M. (2021). Intergenerational equity in sustainable development treaty implementation. In M.-C. C. Segger, M. Szabo, & A. R. Harrington (Eds.), *Intergenerational justice in sustainable development treaty implementation. Advancing future generations rights through national institutions* (pp. 781–791). Cambridge University Press.

Tiihonen, P. (2021). Power over coming generations: Committee for the future in the eduskunta, the parliament of Finland. In M.-C. C. Segger, M. Szabo, & A. R. Harrington (Eds.), *Intergenerational justice in sustainable development treaty implementation. Advancing future generations rights through national institutions* (pp. 395–410). Cambridge University Press.

Tremmel, J. (2014). Nachhaltigkeit. In D. Sturma (Ed.), *Handbuch Bioethik* (pp. 109–114). J.B. Metzler.

Tremmel, J. (2015). Parliaments and future generations: The four-power model. In D. Birnbacher, & M. Thorseth (Eds.), *The politics of sustainability. Philosophical perspectives* (pp. 212–233). Routledge.

Tremmel, J. (2018). Zukunftsräte zur Vertretung der Interessen kommender Generationen. Ein praxisorientierter Vorschlag für Deutschland. In T. Mannewitz (Ed.), *Die Demokratie und ihre Defekte* (pp. 107–142). Springer.

Tremmel, J. (2021). The four-branches model of government: Representing future generations. In M.-C. C. Segger, M. Szabo, & A. R. Harrington (Eds.), *Intergenerational justice in sustainable development treaty implementation. Advancing future generations rights through national institutions* (pp. 754–780). Cambridge University Press.

UN Agenda 21. (1992). United Nations conference on environment & development Rio de Janeiro, Brazil, 3 to 14 June 1992. Agenda 21, paragraph 8.7. Retrieved 02.05.2024 from https://sustainabledevelopment.un.org/content/documents/Agenda21.pdf

UN General Assembly. (2020). UN general assembly. Human rights council, forty-third session, 24 February–20 March 2020 agenda item 3. Visit to Norway. Retrieved 24.04.2024 from https://www.nhri.no/wp-content/uploads/2020/03/Rapport-fra-FNs-spesialrapportør-for-miljø-2020.doc.pdf

UN Report Johannesburg. (2002). Report of the world summit on sustainable development Johannesburg, South Africa, 26 August–4 September 2002. Retrieved 25.04.2024 from https://digitallibrary.un.org/record/478154?v=pdf#files

UN Secretary-General. (2013). Intergenerational solidarity and the needs of future generations. Report of the Secretary-General. United Nations general assembly. Sixty-eighth session. 5 August. Retrieved 30.04.2024 from https://digitallibrary.un.org/record/756820?v=pdf

Vermassen, D., Caluwaerts, D., & Erzeel, S. (2023). Speaking for the voiceless? Representative claims-making on behalf of future generations in Belgium. *Parliamentary Affairs*, 76, 579–599.

WBGU. (2024). Wissenschaftlicher beirat der bundesregierung globale umweltveränderungen. German advisory council on global change. Retrieved 15.04.2024 from https://www.wbgu.de/en/the-wbgu/current-members-of-the-council

Wright, D., & McKenzie, J. (2021). Canadian commissioner of the environment and sustainable development. In M.-C. C. Segger, M. Szabo, & A. R. Harrington (Eds.), *Intergenerational justice in sustainable development treaty implementation. Advancing future generations rights through national institutions* (pp. 461–477). Cambridge University Press.

7

CONSTITUTIONS, PROTECTION CLAUSES, AND CLIMATE LAWSUITS

Introduction

National constitutions stand above all other laws, and no other law within the nation states can contradict them. Most constitutions are difficult to change, and they set a framework for day-to-day political decisions. Constitutions are self-imposed political and legal bindings for current and future generations, and they are the modern states' most important intergenerational contracts (Gosseries, 2008; 2014; Häberle, 2006). Some countries have included protection clauses for future generations in their constitutions. They have thereby committed themselves to binding decisions which are important for the future. These protection clauses are put to the test through climate lawsuits. This chapter discusses whether and how protection clauses in constitutions can ensure that future generations are included in current policy, and how binding they are in practice.

This chapter raises three questions that are extracted from the concept of solidarity with future generations, corresponding to the other empirical chapters, as discussed in Chapter 4. (i) What do the *commitments* by including protection clauses for future generations in national constitutions involve? (ii) How *binding* are these protection clauses for practical policy? (iii) What other societal concerns are in *tension* with the institutional constraint followed by the protection clauses for future generations?

Germany and Norway are analysed as examples of countries that have included a protection clause for future generations in their constitutions, which have been followed by climate lawsuits. The purpose is to conduct political analyses of the arguments concerning future generations used by the four

DOI: 10.4324/9781003400806-9
This chapter has been made available under a CC-BY-NC-ND 4.0 license.

types of participants in the climate lawsuits: complainants, parliaments, governments, and judges in the courts.

The first section of this chapter clarifies what protection clauses are and the differences between the legal processes in Germany and Norway and sources used for the analyses of each country case. The second section presents an overview of legal climate conflicts concerning children and young people worldwide. Most documents used in this overview are retrieved from the Sabin Center's Global Climate Litigation Databases. There are also documents from organisations such as the Urgenda Foundation, Global Legal Action Network, Our Children's Trust, and European Network of National Human Rights Institutions. Most documents are unofficial translations into English, published by the participating actors. The third and fourth sections analyse the German protection clause and the climate lawsuit, while the fifth and sixth sections examine the Norwegian case. The seventh section discusses how these climate lawsuits have shaped new political spaces and frames.

Constitutions and the role of climate lawsuits

In a study of sustainability and law in the Anthropocene, Sjåfjell (2023) argues law is a social construction, which can be seen as a society's most powerful tool to secure social foundation for all contemporary people and for the future, but this requires them to be followed up in practice. The protection clauses in constitutions are based on an underlying social norm that the issues they cover are so essential to consider that they must have a special status in the constitutional democracy. Protection clauses can ensure the rights of future generations, but this varies, as we shall see, between countries and the interpretations of the clauses.

According to Tremmel (2006), around 30 countries have included ecological protection clauses for future generations in their constitutions. A study by Dirth (2018) shows that 120 countries have clauses referring to the environment and sustainability, and 37 explicitly point to future generations. By including protection clauses, the current generations have committed themselves to considering future people in contemporary decision-making. We can distinguish between three types of protection clauses. (i) General clauses refer to general considerations of future conditions of prosperity but not specifically to future generations. (ii) Financial clauses mean one should not transfer debt to future generations. (iii) Ecological clauses point directly to ensuring ecological conditions for those who come after us (Tremmel, 2006).

Germany and Norway have introduced ecological protection clauses. The two countries' constitutions, courts, and lawsuits differ in terms of legal processes, themes, and the issues of the complaints. Despite these differences, they are interesting to compare because both countries have climate lawsuits in which children and young people take their governments to court. One lawsuit in each country is selected where the complainants are children and young people who are concerned for future generations. This is neither meant to be a legal analysis nor a complete evaluation of climate lawsuits. Several legal aspects of the lawsuits are not included in the following analysis, and this applies in particular to discussions of procedures for case management. The focus is on how the subject of future generations is treated in climate lawsuits.

The German case is a political analysis of how the arguments for future generations are included in the climate lawsuit: Neubauer et al. v. Germany. The study covers the constitutional complaint by teenagers and young adults (Neubauer et al. Constitutional complaint, 2020) and the judgement made by the German Federal Constitutional Court (2021). The arguments from the German Government and Parliament (Bundestag) are included in the decisions made by the Federal Constitutional Court, and the analysis of the arguments used by the politicians is based on the court's rendering (Constitutional Court, 2021, Para. 67–69).

The political analysis of the Norwegian case concentrates on how the arguments for future generations are included in the climate lawsuit: Greenpeace Nordic and Nature and Youth Norway v. Ministry of Petroleum and Energy. In contrast to the German case, the Supreme Court of Norway is not a constitutional court. The Norwegian complainants presented their complaint first in the Oslo District Court (2018) and then in the Borgarting Court of Appeal (2020). The environmental organisations were unsuccessful in these courts, and the case was filed with the Supreme Court of Norway. The following analysis of the lawsuit is based on previous studies of the theme (Takle, 2021; 2023), which include main documents from the complainants in the environmental organisations represented by Greenpeace Norden Association (Greenpeace Nordic) and Nature and Youth Norway, the government representation in court by the Office of the Attorney General of Norway, the Oslo District Court, the Borgarting Court of Appeal, and the Supreme Court.

Global trend of climate litigations

There is a global trend of increasing numbers of climate litigations. According to Setzer and Higham (2022; 2023) from the 1980s to 2023 a total of 2,341 climate litigations were registered worldwide. Around two-thirds of the cases have been filed since 2015, which was the year of the Paris Agreement. While they find that the growth rate in cases appears to be slowing, the diversity in cases is still expanding.

This high number of litigations encompasses a broad range of legal procedures and strategies, including lawsuits. While lawsuits refer to the actual dispute between the parties, litigations refer to the procedure of handling a lawsuit. This can involve alternative dispute resolution methods such as mediation and arbitration pretrial motions, evidentiary hearings, and appeals.

Most litigations have occurred in the United States of America (USA) where 1,522 cases are registered. In all other countries outside the USA, 658 cases have been registered in 65 different jurisdictions (Burger & Tigre, 2023). The cases in the Global North represent 89% of the total number of climate litigation cases, including the USA, while cases in the Global South amount to 5.2%. International and regional cases such as the European Court of Human Rights (ECtHR) amount to 5.8% of the climate litigation cases worldwide (Burger & Tigre, 2023).

Climate litigations are ways to force authorities and corporate actors to pursue more ambitious measures to reduce environmental damage. As the measures taken are still insufficient to achieve the purposes of the Paris Agreement, actors in civil society have turned to various judicial bodies. As Burger and Tigre formulate, "Climate change litigation provides civil society, individuals and others with one possible avenue to address inadequate responses by governments and the private sector to the climate crisis" (Burger & Tigre, 2023, p. 7).

Setzer and Higham (2023) conclude that more than 50% of climate cases have direct judicial outcomes that can be understood as favourable to climate action. Moreover, they suggest that climate cases have significant indirect impacts on decision-making beyond the courtroom. An increasing number of cases involve complainants aiming to bring about a more comprehensive social change, such as promoting a new climate policy, creating public awareness, or changing the behaviour of authorities or industrial actors (Setzer & Higham, 2022; 2023).

According to Setzer and Higham (2023) the Urgenda Foundation v. State of the Netherlands from 2019 is the first case in the world where citizens established that their government had a legal duty to prevent dangerous climate change. In 2015, the District Court of The Hague ruled that the government must cut its greenhouse gas emissions by at least 25% by the end of 2020, compared to 1990 levels. On 20 December 2019, the Dutch Supreme Court, the highest court in the Netherlands, upheld this decision. The ruling required the government to reduce emissions in line with its human rights obligations. As a result, the Dutch government closed a power plant four years earlier than planned and introduced a new climate plan in 2019 (Urgenda Foundation, 2023).

Climate lawsuits have become an instrument used by children and youths against governments. In these cases, domestic constitutional protections for the right to a healthy environment play a critical role along with domestic climate legislation (Setzer & Higham, 2023).

Cases where children and young people sue their governments for not adhering to laws laid down in constitutions and in climate and environmental laws and policy are relevant in our context. By the end of 2022, the Sabin Centre databases had registered 34 cases that had been brought by and on behalf of children and young people, defined as people below 25 years of age (Burger & Tigre, 2023).

Children and young people sue their governments for failing to protect their and future generations' lives and health. The cases have an emphasis on the role of human rights. These cases rely on young peoples' particular vulnerability to climate change and the principle of intergenerational equity. This vulnerability is confirmed by Hickman et al. (2021). They found that climate anxiety is widespread among children and young people worldwide and affects their daily functioning. The study was based on a survey of 10,000 children and young people aged 16–25 in 10 countries worldwide in 2021. The authors found that dissatisfaction with government responses to climate change was associated with increased distress. They conclude that climate change has important implications for the health and future of children and young people. Since children and young people have little economic and political power to limit the damage, Hickman et al. (2021) argue this makes them extra vulnerable to climate anxiety.

In the USA, the association *Our Children's Trust* plays an important role. This is a not-for-profit law firm representing young people and their legal right to a healthy atmosphere and a safe climate. While this association has represented children and young people in many lawsuits, one of the most important lawsuits is Held v. State in Montana. On 14 August 2023, Montana Trial Court ruled that the state of Montana violates its citizens' rights to a clean and healthful environment when it grants permits to the fossil-fuel industry. According to Our Children's Trust (2023) this was the first time in US history a court ruled on the merits of a case that the government violated the constitutional rights of children – through laws and actions that promote fossil fuels, ignore climate change, and disproportionately imperil young people. Sixteen young people aged 5–22 were behind the lawsuit. In Montana, the coal industry brings in millions of dollars of revenue every year, and the lawsuit has proved especially contentious among the many people who work in the coal industry. The state is currently appealing the ruling (Held v. State, 2023).

European Court of Human Rights

International and regional courts play an increasing role in the development of jurisprudence. The relationship between harmful climate change and human rights is central (Sandvig, 2021). In 2023, the ECtHR considered four cases as "impact cases" which are deemed a priority for hearing. These are *KlimaSeniorinnen v. Switzerland*, *Careme v. France*, *Duarte Agostinho et al. v. Portugal and 32 Others*, and *Greenpeace Nordic and Others v. Norway*. This development underlines the high profile the court is giving these cases. On 9 April 2024, the ECtHR delivered Grand Chamber rulings in the three first climate change cases (ECtHR, 2024). As of April 2024, the Norwegian case is pending.

In the first case, *Verein KlimaSeniorinnen Schweiz and Others v. Switzerland*, four women and a Swiss association were the complainants. They were concerned about the consequences of global warming on their living conditions and health and argued that the Swiss authorities are not taking sufficient action. The court found that Article 8 of the Convention encompasses a right to effective protection by the State authorities. It concludes that anthropogenic climate change exists, and that it poses a serious current and future threat to the enjoyment of human rights guaranteed under the Convention.

> It noted that current global mitigation efforts are not sufficient to meet that target. It also noted that, while the legal obligations arising for States under the Convention extend to those individuals currently alive who, at a given time, fall within the jurisdiction of a given Contracting Party, it is clear that future generations are likely to bear an increasingly severe burden of the consequences of present failures and omissions to combat climate change.
>
> *(ECtHR 087, 2024, p. 4)*

The court concluded that the Swiss Confederation had failed to comply with its duties under the Convention concerning climate change. It argued that states have a responsibility to protect people from harmful climate change and that they must have good frameworks to ensure emission cuts and concrete plans to implement these goals. The court balances the relationship between law and politics by emphasising that it is up to the politicians to decide which concrete measures should be taken to cut emissions. This will have consequences for how the ECtHR judges future climate lawsuits, such as the Norwegian case.

In the second case, *Carême v. France*, the complainant is a French mayor who claims that his state is not doing enough to protect his right to life, privacy, and property in the face of the risk of a sea level rise in the French coastal town of Grande-Synthe. The ECtHR rejected the application.

In the third case, *Duarte Agostinho et al. v. Portugal and 32 Others*, six young Portuguese, aged 11–24, filed a lawsuit against 32 governments, including 27 EU member states, Norway, Russia, Switzerland, Turkey, and the United Kingdom. The youths filed the case directly with ECtHR without exhausting domestic remedies. They claimed that their fundamental human rights are being violated because of governments' reluctance to fight climate change. The youths were represented by a British law firm, as well as the Irish Legal Activist Organisation, Global Legal Action Network (GLAN, 2023). The ECtHR rejected the application. One reason was that the complainants had not pursued any legal avenue in Portugal concerning their complaints. Another reason was as follows:

> As concerned the extraterritorial jurisdiction of the respondent States other than Portugal, the Court found that there were no grounds in the

> Convention for the extension, by way of judicial interpretation, of their extraterritorial jurisdiction in the manner requested by the applicants.
>
> *(ECtHR, 2024, p. 1)*

This was in line with the respondent states submission to the Grand Chamber ECtHR. Thirty-one of them submitted a joint submission to the Grand Chamber ECtHR in which they argued that climate policy is outside the ECtHR's jurisdiction. "The applicants' approach not only goes far beyond the intended role of the court under the Convention system but is also inconsistent with the internationally agreed framework for combatting climate change which is binding on all of the respondent States" (Respondent States submission to the Grand Chamber ECtHR, 2023, p. 3).

Both the ECtHR and the respondent states defend a global order where sovereign nation states are responsible for climate measures regulated by international climate and environmental agreements. The Portuguese youths argued that indirect reciprocity with people across national borders would lead to cosmopolitan institutional bindings, but this was rejected.

Protection clause in the German Basic Law

The Basic Law (*Grundgesetz*) was established in West Germany in 1949 and has applied to the Federal Republic of Germany since the reunification of 1990. The first 19 articles of the Basic Law contain fundamental rights. In Article 20, the principles of democracy, republicanism, social responsibility, federalism, and the rule of law are laid down in the Basic Law.

The Basic Law can be amended by a two-thirds majority of the German parliament (*Bundestag*) and the Federal Council (*Bundesrat*). Such changes are not allowed to remove any of the principles underlying Articles 1 and 20 as defined by the eternity clause (*Ewigkeitsklausel*) in Article 79 (3). There may be changes to clarify, extend, or refine the fundamental rights in Articles 1–19. However, Articles 1–20 have been amended over time. The eternity clause does not protect any additional words and phrases, as they may be further amended or removed through the normal constitutional process.

In October 1994, Article 20a was added with precise wording about responsibility for future generations. In 2002, the protection of animals was added after discussions regarding the prohibition of ritual slaughter (dejure.org, 2023). Article 20a of the German Basic Law states:

> Mindful also of its responsibility toward future generations, the state shall protect the natural foundations of life and animals by legislation and, in accordance with law and justice, by executive and judicial action, all within the framework of the constitutional order.
>
> *(Ministry of Justice, 2023)*

The fact that the article came close to Articles 1–19 underlines its relevance to fundamental rights. However, the introduction as a policy objective of the state implies a different quality (Tremmel, 2022; Weiss, 2021).

German climate lawsuit

In February 2020, a group of nine German youths and young adults, aged 15–33 years, filed a case to the Federal Constitutional Court (Neubauer et al. v. Germany, 2021). This was filed at the same time as three other groups of claimants who were all targeting the government's climate protection measures. (i) Friends of the Earth Germany (BUND) and the Association of Solar Supporters and Others in November 2018; (ii) Yi Yi Prue and other individuals from Bangladesh and Nepal in January 2020; (iii) Steinmetz and other individual German youths in January 2020. The following analysis concentrates on the arguments concerning future generations in Neubauer et al. v. Germany.

The youths and young adults claimed that the provisions of the Federal Climate Change Act (*Bundesklimaschutzgesetz*) were insufficient, and that the legislator therefore had violated their human rights as protected by the Basic Law. With this act the federal government committed itself to achieving a greenhouse gas reduction of 55% by 2030 and then extensive decarbonisation by 2050. This target, the youths argued, does not consider the findings of science and the reports from the Intergovernmental Panel on Climate Change (IPCC), and it does not consider Germany's and the EU's obligation under the Paris Agreement to limit global temperature increase to well below 2°C and, if possible, to 1.5°C compared to pre-industrial levels. Moreover, the Climate Change Act does not have a reduction path after 2030 (Neubauer et al. Constitutional complaint, 2020).

The young peoples' claims were that the targets of the Federal Climate Change Act have led to violations of their fundamental right to a future consistent with human dignity and their basic right to life and physical integrity, as enshrined in Articles 1 and 2 of the Basic Law, and in conjunction with Article 20a of the Basic Law. Moreover, they argued that "State action or omissions must not destroy the foundations of the self-development of others and the preservation of the conditions of existence of future generations" (Neubauer et al. Constitutional complaint, 2020, p. 7). Some of the youths also claimed to be violated in their freedom of occupation and under their freedom of ownership.

The complainants presented themselves as young people who do not reach through the democratic channel and, thereby, feel helpless.

> The complainants are between 15 and 32 years old and are hence expected to experience all the predicted effects of climate change by the turn of

> the century. They are already affected by the noticeable effects of climate change in Germany (e.g. extreme weather conditions, heat waves), but cannot protect themselves through their democratic rights, especially not through voting. They feel helplessly exposed to the economic and political "business as usual" and are under considerable stress with regard to their own future.
>
> *(Neubauer et al. Constitutional complaint, 2020, pp. 11–12)*

The youths asked the Federal Constitutional Court to declare that the German legislature violated their rights in the Basic Law by the low reduction of greenhouse gas by 2030 in the Federal Climate Change Act. Moreover, they asked the court to declare that the legislature was required to issue new reduction quotas to ensure that Germany's emissions are kept as low as possible, taking into account the principle of proportionality. Finally, the young people asked the court to declare that Germany is prohibited from transferring emissions allocations to neighbouring European states. The latter applies as long as the common European climate protection legislation does not provide a level of protection sufficient for fundamental rights (Neubauer et al. Constitutional complaint, 2020).

In contrast, the *Bundestag* and the federal government argued that the constitutional complaints were inadmissible and unfounded (Constitutional Court, 2021, Para. 67–69). The *Bundestag* argued that the alignment with the remaining CO_2 budget results from an evaluation of democratic processes and cannot be derived from fundamental rights (Constitutional Court, 2021, Para. 67–68). The federal government considered that it does not appear that the complainants' fundamental rights were violated by the government's alleged omission. Moreover, it argued that the principle of human dignity in conjunction with Article 20a of the Basic Law implies an obligation for the state to guarantee living conditions that already exist today, and this cannot be carried forward into the future. The government believed that this was foreign to German constitutional law (Constitutional Court, 2021, Para. 69).

German Federal Constitutional Court's decision

The complainants filed their challenge directly to the German Federal Constitutional Court (*Bundesverfassungsgericht*). The Constitutional Court is the guardian of the Basic Law. It is an independent constitutional organ which monitors and assures compliance with the Basic Law, and it only hears constitutional cases.

On 29 April 2021, the Federal Constitutional Court published its decision on the case. The court decided jointly on this complaint along with the three other groups of claimants who were targeting the government's climate protection measures, as mentioned earlier (Constitutional Court, 2021).

The following analysis concentrates on the court's arguments concerning future generations in the case Neubauer et al. v. Germany, although some arguments overlap. The Constitutional Court's decision on this case was announced as a partial success for the complainants. The court concluded that the provisions of the Federal Climate Change Act are incompatible with fundamental rights. The main reason is that the act lacks specifications for further emission reductions from 2031 onwards. The other parts of the complaints were rejected.

Two aspects of the court's reasoning are of particular importance regarding social solidarity with future generations. Firstly, the court had an intergenerational approach including future generations. It argued that the Climate Change Act irreversibly leaves significant emission reduction burdens to periods after 2030. These burdens will, the court stated, expose the young and subsequent generations to comprehensive losses of freedom in the future.

> When Art. 20a GG obliges the state to protect the natural foundations of life – partly out of responsibility towards future generations – it is aimed first and foremost at preserving the natural foundations of life for future generations. But at the same time, it also concerns how environmental burdens are spread between different generations.
>
> *(Constitutional Court, Para. 193)*

The Constitutional Court argued that Article 20a of the Basic Law not only obliges the legislature to protect the climate and aim towards achieving climate neutrality but also concerns how environmental burdens are spread out between different generations. It described the fundamental rights as intertemporal guarantees of freedom,

> (…) one generation must not be allowed to consume large portions of the CO_2 budget while bearing a relatively minor share of the reduction effort, if this would involve leaving subsequent generations with a drastic reduction burden and expose their lives to serious losses of freedom.
>
> *(Constitutional Court, Press Release No. 31/2021)*

It emphasised that the consequences of today's actions lie in the future and that this fact must have consequences for current legal practice and politics. Formulated the opposite way, individuals' fundamental rights to freedom in the future lie in the present. With these arguments, the court applies indirect reciprocity with future generations. It not only draws attention to future generations in today's politics but also includes them in the political community as equal parties who should enjoy the same basic freedoms as today's generations. This means that Article 20a in the Basic Law entails a specific duty of care in relation to future generations (Kirchmair, 2023;

Tremmel, 2022). Accordingly, Colombo (2023) uses this case as an example to show how courts can offer practical ways to increase the political space for future freedoms (Colombo, 2023).

Secondly, the court stated that the fact that no state can resolve the problems of climate change on its own does not invalidate the national obligation to take climate action. It argued that Article 20a makes it obligatory to take national climate action in cases where international cooperation does not lead to legally formalised agreements.

> It is true that Germany would not be capable of preventing climate change on its own. Its isolated activity is clearly not the only causal factor determining the progression of climate change and the effectiveness of climate action. Climate change can only be stopped if climate neutrality is achieved worldwide. In view of the global reduction requirements, Germany's 2% share of worldwide CO_2 emissions (...) is only a small factor. Still, if Germany's climate action measures are embedded within global efforts, they are capable of playing a part in the overall drive to bring climate change to a halt.
>
> *(Constitutional Court, 2021, Para. 202)*

According to the court, dependence on the international community gives rise to a constitutional necessity for a state to carry out its climate measures at the national level. By requiring the natural basis of life to be protected for future generations, the court argued that the protection clause makes it obligatory to pursue a goal that can only be achieved through supranational and international cooperation.

Moreover, the court emphasised that precisely because of the state's dependencies on international cooperation to effectively carry out its obligation to take climate action according to Article 20a in the Basic Law, the state must avoid creating incentives for other states to undermine this cooperation: "In practice, resolving the global climate problem is thus largely dependent on the existence of mutual trust that others will also strive to achieve the targets" (Constitutional Court, 2021, Para. 203). The aim for the court is to prevent other states from undermining this cooperation. Although the court emphasises that each country must take responsibility for its emissions, this is seen globally, where the countries depend on cooperation.

The Constitutional Court concluded that the legislators had to adopt provisions by 31 December 2022. This involved a specification of the provisions for reduction targets from 2031 onwards. This ruling is binding on German policymakers. In response, federal policymakers passed a law that immediately steps up the goals of a 65% reduction in greenhouse gases from 1990 levels by 2030 and redefined the sector-specific annual emission levels for 2023–2030 and the yearly cross-sector reduction targets for 2031–2040.

It has been in effect since August 2021 (Bundestag, 2021). This places greater efforts on people living today.

The Constitutional Court provides rights to future generations in a way that binds today's actions. Its arguments can be interpreted in terms of indirect reciprocity combined with cosmopolitan solidarity, placing great emphasis on supranational cooperation. Germany must act to not undermine international and supranational cooperation. This shows a gradual shift in the argument towards increased solidarity with future generations.

Protection clause in the Norwegian Constitution

The Norwegian Constitution (*Grunnlov*) of 1814 is the second oldest constitution which is still in force. An amendment to the Constitution requires a two-thirds majority in the Norwegian parliament (*Storting*) and changes can only be adopted after a new election. Many of the provisions of the Norwegian Constitution are relatively short and aim to specify general rules (Fauchald & Smith, 2019). This also applies to the environmental protection clause, Article 112 of the Norwegian Constitution, which states:

> Every person has the right to an environment that is conducive to health and to a natural environment whose productivity and diversity are maintained. Natural resources shall be managed on the basis of comprehensive long-term considerations which will safeguard this right for future generations as well.
>
> In order to safeguard their right in accordance with the foregoing paragraph, citizens are entitled to information on the state of the natural environment and on the effects of any encroachment on nature that is planned or carried out.
>
> The authorities of the state shall take measures for the implementation of these principles.
>
> *(Stortinget, 2018)*

In 1992, the first version of the protection clause, Article 110b, was included in the constitution. In 2014, Article 110b was revised and moved to Article 112 and simultaneously included in a new human rights chapter in the constitution. These changes were a part of a larger revision of the Norwegian Constitution with the Constitution's 200th anniversary in 2014 (Fauchald & Smith, 2019). To prepare this revision, the *Storting* appointed a commission. Regarding the environmental provision, this commission proposed to keep paragraphs 1 and 2 of Article 112 as they were, while sharpening the wording in paragraph three (Dokument 16 (2011–2012)). This sharpening implied changes from the State authorities, ranging from "shall issue further provisions" to "it is incumbent on the state authorities to take measures." The purpose of this change was to clarify that the authorities have an active duty to safeguard a healthy environment for current and future generations through various forms of measures (Dokument 16 (2011–2012), pp. 244–246). In 2014, the *Storting* decided to follow these recommendations almost without debate (Innst. 187 S (2013–2014)).

Norwegian climate lawsuit

In October 2016, Greenpeace Nordic and Nature and Youth Norway (*Natur og Ungdom*) took legal action against the Norwegian Government for violating the Constitution's Article 112 (Greenpeace Nordic and Nature and Youth Norway v. Ministry of Petroleum and Energy (People v Arctic Oil), 2016). The central issue was the Norwegian government's decision from 10 June 2016 on awarding licences to search for petroleum in the Barents Sea. Due to climate change and the vulnerability of areas in the High North, environmental organisations contended the country should not search for more petroleum in these areas and should also phase out petroleum production (Greenpeace Nordic and Nature and Youth Norway, 2020).

The environmental organisations perceived Article 112 as a rights provision. In terms of rights, they also argued that the decision on awarding production licences is contrary to the European Convention on Human Rights. Moreover, they argued that the threshold should be low when the courts are to set limits for democratic decisions, and in this case, they claimed it was already exceeded. An overall assessment of environmental harm must, according to the environmental organisations, include risks involved in an environmentally valuable area connected to the polar front and the ice edge, and the emission of greenhouse gases in connection with production and combustion. They referred to the established knowledge of how serious the climate crisis already is and argued that future generations' access to a healthy environment is decisive for defining a low threshold (Greenpeace Nordic and Nature and Youth Norway, 2016, 2018, 2019, 2020).

Moreover, the environmental organisations contended that the Norwegian *Storting's* discretion is strictly limited due to both legal and factual circumstances, and the concern for future generations is crucial.

> Because future generations lack the opportunity to safeguard their own need for a liveable environment, Article 112 of the Norwegian Constitution protects precisely these "future generations." This is essential when determining the discretion, which must be narrowed if the concern for "future generations" requires it.
>
> *(Greenpeace Nordic and Nature and Youth Norway, 2020, p. 6)*

The organisations' arguments can be understood in terms of indirect reciprocity with future generations. They argued that today's generations must act in a way that makes it possible for the people of the future to develop their capabilities. Their central concern was that there is no room for more fossil-fuel resources if future generations should have access to a healthy environment to be able to enhance their capabilities. The decision to search for petroleum will have a serious environmental impact, which cannot be justified on the basis of economic considerations (Greenpeace Nordic and Nature and Youth Norway, 2020).

According to the environmental organisations one should not only assess the environmental damage associated with oil and gas production in Norway. The assessments should also include greenhouse gas emissions related to combustion outside Norway from oil and gas produced in Norway. The argument was that in a situation of catastrophic global warming, Norway has a global responsibility that must be assessed because the country is a significant oil exporter (Greenpeace Nordic and Nature and Youth Norway, 2020). By emphasising the Norwegian responsibility for the future worldwide, the organisations included aspects of cosmopolitan solidarity. This is in the form that every nation state is responsible for the territorial harm caused by the combustion of emissions from fossil fuels extracted from its territory, as discussed earlier.

In contrast, none of the main documents from the government has references to future generations (Attorney General of Norway, 2016; 2018; 2020). The government's point of departure was that this article does not provide substantive rights for individuals which can be reviewed before the courts. It meant that decisions on awarding production licences involve political decisions that should be made by elected representatives in the Norwegian *Storting* and not by the courts. Moreover, the government argued politically that the protection clause is neither suited to, nor intended for, any regulation of greenhouse gas emissions and it cannot be understood to set limits for Norwegian petroleum exports (Attorney General of Norway, 2016).

Moreover, the government argued that emissions from the combustion of Norwegian petroleum outside Norwegian jurisdiction are not covered by Article 112. It stated that the constitution does not provide global rights and has a limited scope of application and jurisdiction in terms of persons and territory. The government referred to the fact that international and national climate policies are based on each state being responsible for its national emissions, and Norway has committed itself to reducing its emissions through international agreements such as the Paris Agreement (Attorney General of Norway, 2020). It contended the emissions from the new fields in the Barents Sea are uncertain and will be marginal in a global perspective. With this, it argued the opposite of the German Constitutional Court, which claimed that no state can evade its responsibility, no matter how little it contributes to climate change.

The conflict between the environmental organisations and the government should be seen in light of what Chapters 1 and 6 discussed as the Norwegian paradox. In this climate lawsuit, petroleum activities, the country's most profitable industry, are set against climate change, which is one of the most critical environmental challenges the world is facing (Ytterstad et al., 2022). The Norwegian welfare state is dependent on income from its large petroleum industry. Therefore, this climate lawsuit reveals how long-term concern for protecting the environment for future generations is in tension with challenges to today's welfare state.

Supreme Court of Norway's decision

The Supreme Court rejected the appeal in December 2020. Most of the judges voted in favour of the Norwegian state. Four of the 15 judges argued the decision on awarding licences was invalid due to procedural errors, and they believed further processing of the case in relation to future global emissions of greenhouse gases was necessary. Regarding future generations, one central conclusion was that Article 112 only allows for judicial review under limited circumstances, and these were not fulfilled in this case. The wording in Article 112 reflects an intermediate solution between a substantive right and a declaration of principle (Supreme Court, 2020). This implies, the court concluded, there is a substantive right to limit governmental actions, but only when the *Storting* has not taken a position on an environmental problem. The court held that the threshold must be high for when the court is to set limits for democratic decisions. It called Article 112 a "safety valve" for circumstances where the *Storting* has neither considered environmental problems nor implemented measures (Supreme Court, 2020, Para. 142).

The Supreme Court did not define any criteria for where to place the threshold but described Article 112 as providing a guidance to lawmakers and administrative decision-making. By referring to the balance between the rule of law and democracy, the court concluded in line with the government that environmental issues include broad assessments, and such decisions should be made by elected bodies and not by the courts (Supreme Court, 2020). While the court recognised the severity of climate change and the legal importance of the Paris Agreement, none of these considerations seems to have relevance for how it interpreted Article 112 (Voigt, 2021). Moreover, the court held that the link between the decision to grant oil production licences in the Barents Sea and an increase in climate gas emissions is too uncertain to violate the human rights in line with the European Convention of Human Rights Articles 2 and 8.

Like the government, the Supreme Court concluded that Norwegian climate policy is based on the division of responsibility between nation states which comply with international agreements. The court rejected the environmental organisations' claim that Article 112 provides protection outside Norway associated with combustion of oil and gas produced in Norway.

The tension illuminated in this lawsuit is evident in the Supreme Court's argument that the environmental organisations' position would imply that central parts of Norwegian petroleum policy, including extraction and export, were put to the test. Moreover, it argued that the organisations' position would affect later licensing rounds and thereby involve a controlled phasing out of Norwegian petroleum activities. According to the Supreme Court this is outside the scope of what the court could rule on (Supreme Court, 2020).

Based on this case, we can conclude that the protection clause in the constitution has a weak binding on today's political decision-makers to consider future generations. As Voigt (2021) argues, the court failed to fulfil its mandate to hold the government accountable to its constitutional responsibilities. It is thereby up to the elected politicians in the *Storting* to decide what today's generations should do with petroleum production. So far, there is a broad political consensus in favour of increased production of oil and gas.

Follow-up of the climate lawsuit in Norway

In December 2021, the two organisations together with six young Norwegians appealed the climate lawsuit by bringing the case before the ECtHR (Greenpeace Nordic and Others v. Norway, 2021). They claimed that the Norwegian state violates their fundamental human rights, under Articles 2 (right to life) and 8 (right to respect for private life and family life and home) of the European Convention on Human Rights, by issuing new oil-drilling licences in the Arctic.

The ECtHR has characterised the case as a potential "impact case" and requested the Norwegian Government to respond to the application. In April 2022, the Norwegian state asked the ECtHR to dismiss the case or to find that there had been no violation. In its reply, the state argued that the Russian invasion of Ukraine justifies the search for more oil and gas today, thus increasing greenhouse gas emissions for another 30 years or more (Greenpeace Nordic and Others v. Norway, 2021). As of March 2024, the case has the status of pending.

The case has also been followed up by the Norwegian Human Rights Institution (NIM), which is an independent institution established to strengthen the implementation of human rights in Norway by the Constitution, the Human Rights Act and international human rights law. In 2022, NIM sent a report to the Ministry of Petroleum and Energy, in which it referred to the Supreme Court's decision from 2020 (NIM, 2022). According to NIM the court argued that the state has a duty under Article 112 to refuse to approve a Plan for Development and Operation (POD) of a petroleum deposit when consideration of the climate and the environment otherwise dictates it. Such assessments should include both national and exported combustion emissions. NIM argued that the state has a duty to refuse to approve such plans when approval gives rise to combustion which is incompatible with limiting global warming to 1.5°C. Correspondingly, NIM (2022) argued that future generations' right to a liveable climate must be integrated into the ministry's assessments.

In a new lawsuit in 2023, the environmental organisations Greenpeace Nordic and Nature and Youth Norway (*Natur og Ungdom*) challenged the validity of the government's approvals of plans for the development and operation of the oil and gas fields of Breidablikk, Yggdrasil, and Tyrving in the North Sea. The lawsuit was based on several legal sources, and Article 112 was central (Greenpeace Nordic and Nature and Youth v. Energy Ministry, 2023).

In January 2024, the Oslo District Court (2024) decided that the environmental organisations were right on all points. This means that the development of the three new oil and gas fields is invalid and that the development of two of them must cease immediately (Greenpeace Nordic and Nature & Youth v. Energy Ministry, 2023). One of the central disagreements between the environmental organisations and the government concerned how to interpret the Supreme Court's 2020 assessments about when and how to interpret a plan for the development and operation of a POD when consideration of the climate and the environment requires it. Crucial was the question of whether to include the combustion abroad of Norwegian-produced oil and gas in such considerations. The environmental organisations lost in the previous climate lawsuit from 2020 but used the Supreme Court's interpretation of 112 in this case. This was also in line with NIM's assessments as discussed earlier.

Oslo District Court (2024) argued in line with the environmental organisations that before approving oil and gas fields, the state must assess the impact of greenhouse gas emissions resulting from the development and operation of petroleum deposits. This was also NIM's standpoint of how to interpret the Supreme Court's decision. However, the Oslo District Court had no references to future generations. While the environmental organisations claimed that consideration of the best interests of children living today should have been investigated and assessed, the court rejected this. Oslo District Court (2024) concluded that there is no legal obligation to consider children's best interests in connection with each decision on a plan for developing and operating petroleum activities. At the end of January 2024, the state appealed the case.

New political spaces and frames

The German and Norwegian cases are examples of a global trend of an increasing number of climate litigations worldwide. Particularly children and youths are anxious about climate and ecological changes. As they do gain influence through political channels, they try to reach out to change climate and environmental policy through legal systems. As Colombo (2023) argues, legal mobilisations through the courts can constitute a proxy for youth participation as litigations provide a political space where future generations are seen and heard.

By including protection clauses in their constitutions, Germany and Norway have committed the state to consider future generations. These commitments enable children and young people to bring their governments to court, and so they have done. They have used the courtroom to argue that more consideration should be given to future generations.

In both countries, the young claimants referred to the established knowledge of how serious the climate crisis already is, and the importance of future generations' access to a healthy environment. They appealed to intergenerational solidarity based on an equal access to a healthy environment for young people living today and future unborn generations. The German claimants framed themselves as young people who do not reach through the democratic channel, and thereby, feel helpless regarding their own future. The Norwegian claimants argued that future generations lack the opportunity to safeguard their own need for a liveable environment and, therefore, the protection clause in the constitution should protect them. In both countries the claimants' ideas mean that current generations are open to identify with future people and impose institutional constraints on themselves. This implies indirect reciprocity, which has aspects of cosmopolitan ideas.

Conversely, the governments in both countries rejected the legal complaints by pointing out that this is a matter for political institutions. They considered the complaints unacceptable and groundless. None of them saw any reason why the complainants' arguments should lead to changes in policy.

The rulings from the countries' highest courts are decisive for how binding these protection clauses in the countries' constitutions are in practice. The German Federal Constitutional Court's rulings entailed far stronger restrictions on German politics than the Norwegian Supreme Court's judgement had on Norwegian politics.

The German Constitutional Court concluded that the provisions of the Federal Climate Change Act are incompatible with fundamental rights and that the legislators had to change this act. In response, federal policymakers have passed an act that immediately steps up the goals of the current reduction in greenhouse gases. More significant efforts are placed on people living today. From this we can conclude that the protection clause in the German Basic Law has introduced significant institutional bindings.

In contrast, the Supreme Court of Norway called the protection clause in the Norwegian Constitution a "safety valve" for circumstances where the *Storting* has neither considered environmental problems nor implemented measures. Since the court did not apply the safety valve in this case, the protection clause has introduced weak institutional bindings to ensure a healthy environment for future generations.

Both cases reveal a shift in arguments over time. New frames for problem definition and moral evaluations were introduced by the German Federal Constitutional Court. It described the fundamental rights as intertemporal guarantees of freedom and emphasised that the consequences of today's actions lie in the future. According to the court, this fact must have consequences for current legal practice and politics. Moreover, the court stated that dependence on the international community makes it necessary for a state to carry out its national climate measures. Although no state can resolve the problems of climate change on its own, the court argued, this does not invalidate the national obligation to take climate action. With these arguments, we can conclude that the Constitutional Court refers to indirect reciprocity, and its decision is crucial for the implementation of institutional constraints.

In Norway, the introduction of new frames through the lawsuits is slow and more vulnerable. New frames can be revealed in how the Oslo District Court in 2024 interpreted the Supreme Court's 2020 assessments. The Oslo District Court argued in line with the environmental organisations that before approving oil and gas fields, the state must assess the impact of greenhouse gas emissions resulting from the development and operation of petroleum deposits. This also includes the combustion abroad of Norwegian-produced oil and gas in such considerations. However, the judgement from the Oslo District Court made no explicit references to future generations, and there are no indications of new frames that include them. In practice, the ruling could still have consequences for future generations, but the state has appealed the ruling, and the outcome is uncertain.

Regarding tensions, there was far more at stake in the Norwegian climate lawsuit than in the German one. The Supreme Court of Norway confirmed this by stating that the environmental organisations' position would imply that central parts of Norwegian petroleum policy, including extraction and export, were put to the test. The claimants' position would affect later licensing rounds and thereby involve a controlled phasing out of Norwegian petroleum activities, the country's most important source of income. In contrast, the tensions in the German climate lawsuit involved questions about intergenerational burden distribution concerning greenhouse gas emissions. The changes in the Climate Change Act had minor consequences for German politics.

The German and Norwegian lawsuits show that the institutional bindings provided by the protection clauses in constitutions are weak. Still, they have contributed to a gradual shift in the framing of the state's responsibility for future generations. Environmental activists have used the protection clauses to promote new problem definitions, moral evaluations, and measures in the courtroom.

Summary

- There are increasing numbers of climate litigations worldwide, in which children and youths try to reach out to change climate and environmental policy through legal systems.
- The claimants in Germany and Norway refer both to the established knowledge of how serious the climate crisis is and to the commitments in the protection clauses to give future generations access to a healthy environment.
- While the German claimants present themselves as young people who do not reach through the democratic channel, Norwegian environmental organisations argue that the protection clause in the constitution should protect future generations.
- The governments in Germany and Norway rejected the legal complaints by pointing to the fact that these issues involve political decisions that should be made by elected representatives in the parliament and not by the courts.
- The German Federal Constitutional Court concluded that the legislators had to specify the provisions for reduction targets from 2031 onwards, and German policymakers have changed the Climate Change Act.
- The way the German Constitutional Court argued for fundamental rights for future generations and intergenerational sharing of efforts can be interpreted as indirect reciprocity with future generations, which leads to institutional constraints.
- The Supreme Court of Norway called Article 112 a "safety valve" for circumstances where the *Storting* has neither considered environmental problems nor implemented measures, and this was not applied in this case.
- The tensions in the German climate lawsuit concern which generation will carry the efforts of necessary reductions in greenhouse gas emissions.
- The tensions in the Norwegian climate lawsuit are between the petroleum industry as the country's most important industry, and climate change, which is important for protecting the environment for future generations worldwide.
- In both cases, the complainants and the courts have introduced new frames of moral evaluations and problem-solving regarding future generations in the courtrooms and thereby in the public debates.

References

Attorney General of Norway. (2016). Notice of defence to Oslo District Court. Unofficial translation. Retrieved 12.04.2024 from www.klimasøksmål.no/wp-content/uploads/2019/10/Government-Response_unofficial-translation_ENG.pdf

Attorney General of Norway. (2018). Reply to notice of appeal to Supreme Court of Norway. Unofficial translation. Retrieved 12.04.2024 from www.klimasøksmål.no/wp-content/uploads/2019/10/2.-APPEAL-RESPONSE.pdf

Attorney General of Norway. (2020). Anketilsvar til Høyesterett. Date 3 March. Retrieved 12.04.2024 from https://www.klimasøksmål.no/wp-content/uploads/2020/04/2020-03-31-D158-Anketilsvar-Høyesterett-fra-staten.pdf

Borgarting Court of Appeal. (2020). Judgement pronounced 23 January 2020. Case no.: LB-2018-60499. Unofficial translation. Retrieved 21.04.2024 https://www.klimasøksmål.no/wp-content/uploads/2019/10/judgement_Peoplevs_ArcticOil_Appeal_Jan2020.pdf

Bundestag, G. (2021). Erstes Gesetz zur Änderung des Bundes-Klimaschutzgesetzes. Retrieved 13.10.2023 from https://dip.bundestag.de/vorgang/erstes-gesetz-zur-änderung-des-bundes-klimaschutzgesetzes/277959

Burger, M., & Tigre, M. A. (2023). Global climate litigation report: 2023 status review. Sabin Center for Climate Change Law, Columbia Law School & United Nations Environment Programme, 2023. Retrieved 21.04.2024 https://scholarship.law.columbia.edu/sabin_climate_change/202

Colombo, E. (2023). The politics of silence: Hannah Arendt and future generations' fight for the climate. *ICL Journal. Vienna Journal on International Constitutional Law*, *17*(1), 43–81.

Constitutional Court, German Federal. (2021). Bundesverfassungsgerich. BVerfG, Order of the First Senate of 24 March 2021 - 1 BvR 2656/18 -, paras. 1–270. Retrieved 11.10.2023 from https://www.bverfg.de/e/rs20210324_1bvr265618en.html

dejure.org. (2023). Art. 20a Grundgesetz. Grundgesetz Rechtsprechung zu Art. 20a. Retrieved 10.10.2023 from https://dejure.org/gesetze/GG/20a.html

Dirth, E. (2018). *Governance for future generations: A global review of the implementation of intergenerational equity*. Utrecht University Repository. Retrieved 30.04.2024 from https://studenttheses.uu.nl/handle/20.500.12932/28652?show=full

Dokument 16. (2011–2012). Rapport fra Menneskerettighetsutvalget om menneskerettigheter i Grunnloven, avgitt 19. desember 2011. Retrieved 12.04.2024 from https://www.stortinget.no/Global/pdf/Dokumentserien/2011-2012/dok16-201112.pdf

ECtHR. (2024). European Court of Human Rights. Grand Chamber rulings in the climate change cases. Retrieved 09.04.2024 from https://www.echr.coe.int/w/grand-chamber-rulings-in-the-climate-change-cases

ECtHR 087. (2024). European Court of Human Rights. Verein KlimaSeniorinnen Schweiz and Others v. Switzerland. Retrieved 09.04.2024 from https://hudoc.echr.coe.int/eng-press#{%22itemid%22:[%22003-7919428-11026177%22]}

Fauchald, O. K., & Smith, E. (Eds.) (2019). *Mellom jus og politikk. Grunnlovens § 112*. Fagbokforlaget.

GLAN. (2023). GLAN, Global Legal Action Network. Case documents. Retrieved 03.10.2023 from https://youth4climatejustice.org/case-documents/

Gosseries, A. (2008). Constitutions and future generations. *The Good Society*, *17*(2), 32–37.

Gosseries, A. (2014). The intergenerational case for constitutional rigidity. *Ratio Juris*, *27*(4), 528–539.

Greenpeace Nordic and Nature and Youth Norway. (2016). Notice of proceeding in Oslo District Court. 18 October 2016. Unofficial translation. Retrieved 03.05.2024 from https://www.klimasøksmål.no/wp-content/uploads/2019/10/Notice-of-Proceedings-Final-Translation.pdf

Greenpeace Nordic and Nature and Youth Norway. (2018). Direct appeal to the Supreme Court of Norway. Date 5 February 2018. Unofficial translation. Retrieved 03.05.2024 from https://www.klimasøksmål.no/wp-content/uploads/2019/10/1.-APPEAL.pdf

Greenpeace Nordic and Nature and Youth Norway. (2019). Statement of case to Borgarting Court of Appeal. 12 August 2019. Case no: 18-060499ASD-BORG/03. Unofficial translation. Retrieved 03.05.2024 from https://www.klimasøksmål.no/wp-content/uploads/2019/10/Writ-on-international-law-and-proceedural-issues-Aug-2019.pdf

Greenpeace Nordic and Nature and Youth Norway. (2020). Notice of appeal to the Supreme Court of Norway. Date 24 February 2020. Unofficial translation. Retrieved 03.05.2024 from https://drive.google.com/file/d/1Mkjoemyd3XSxpN49YVXz83h9zy87z5Uf/view

Greenpeace Nordic and Nature and Youth v. Energy Ministry. (2023). (The North Sea Fields Case). Challenged three administrative decisions to Oslo District Court. Sabin Center Climate Change Litigation Databases. Retrieved 30.04.2024 from https://climatecasechart.com/non-us-case/the-north-sea-fields-case-greenpeace-nordic-and-nature-youth-v-energy-ministry/

Greenpeace Nordic and Others v. Norway. (2021). Filed an application before the European Court of Human Rights against the Norwegian government. Sabin Center Climate Change Litigation Databases. Retrieved 30.04.2024 from https://climatecasechart.com/non-us-case/greenpeace-nordic-assn-v-ministry-of-petroleum-and-energy-ecthr/

Greenpeace Nordic Ass'n v. Ministry of Petroleum and Energy (People v Arctic Oil). (2016). Sabin Center Climate Change Litigation Databases. Retrieved 17.10.2023 from https://climatecasechart.com/non-us-case/greenpeace-nordic-assn-and-nature-youth-v-norway-ministry-of-petroleum-and-energy/

Häberle, P. (2006). A constitutional law for future generations – The 'other' form of the social contract: The generation contract. In J. Tremmel (Ed.), *Handbook of intergenerational justice* (pp. 215–229). Edward Elgar.

Held v. State. (2023). Montana Trial Court decision. Sabin Center Climate Change Litigation Databases. Retrieved 15.10.2023 from https://climatecasechart.com/case/11091/

Hickman, C., Marks, E., Pihkala. P., Clayton, S., Lewandowski, E., Mayall, E. E., Wray, B., Mellor, C. & van Susteren, L. (2021). Climate anxiety in children and young people and their beliefs about government responses to climate change: A global survey. *Lancet Planetary Health*, 2021(5), 863–873.

Innst. 187 S. (2013–2014). Recommendation to the Storting (2014). Innstilling til Stortinget fra kontroll- og konstitusjonskomiteen. Retrieved 03.05.2024 from https://www.stortinget.no/no/Saker-og-publikasjoner/Publikasjoner/Innstillinger/Stortinget/2013-2014/inns-201314-187/?lvl=0

Kirchmair, L. (2023). Enforcing constitutional sustainability clauses in the age of the climate crisis: Insights from social contract theory on how to take account of future generations. *International Constitutional Law Journal*, *17*(1), 1–16.

Ministry of Justice, German Federal. (2023). Basic Law for the Federal Republic of Germany. Retrieved 10.10.2023 from https://www.gesetze-im-internet.de/englisch_gg/englisch_gg.html

Neubauer et al. Constitutional complaint. (2020). Constitutional complaint by the teenagers and young adults 06.02.2020. Unofficial translation. Retrieved 16.04.2024 from https://climatecasechart.com/wp-content/uploads/non-us-case-documents/2020/20200206_11817_complaint.pdf

Neubauer et al. v. Germany. (2021). Sabin Center Climate Change Litigation Databases. Retrieved 05.10.2023 from https://climatecasechart.com/non-us-case/neubauer-et-al-v-germany/

NIM. (2022). Norwegian National Human Rights Institution. Grunnloven § 112og plan for utbygging og drift av petroleumsforekomster. Til Olje- og energidepartementet. Retrieved 14.03.2024 from https://www.nhri.no/2022/utredning-om-grunnloven-§-112-og-plan-for-utbygging-og-drift-av-petroleumsforekomster/

Oslo District Court. (2018). Oslo District Court judgement. Pronounced 04.01.2018. Case no.: 16-166674tvi-otir/06. Unofficial translation. Retrieved 02.05.2024 from https://www.klimasøksmål.no/wp-content/uploads/2019/10/Judgement-4.-jan-2017-Oslo-District-Court-stamped-version.pdf

Oslo District Court. (2024). Oslo District Court judgement. Pronounced 18.01.2024. Case no.: 23-099330TVI-TOSL/05. Retrieved 02.05.2024 from https://climatecasechart.com/wp-content/uploads/non-us-case-documents/2024/20240118_Application-no.-23-099330TVI-TOSL05_judgment.pdf

Our Children's Trust. (2023). Sweeping constitutional win for Held v. State of Montana youth plaintiffs. Retrieved 06.10.2023 from https://static1.squarespace.com/static/571d109b04426270152febe0/t/64da6d67161d05783fbca2f9/1692036457635/08.14.2023+Montana+Climate+Youth+Win.pdf

Respondent States submission to the Grand Chamber ECtHR. (2023). Duarte Agostinho et al. v. Portugal and 32 Others. Observations of the respondents on admissibility and merits, 31 January 2023. GLAN, Global Legal Action Network. Case documents. Retrieved 09.10.2023 from https://youth4climatejustice.org/case-documents/

Sandvig, J. (2021). Menneskerettigheter og klima. Klimarettssaker. In H. C. Bugge (Ed.), *Klimarett. Internasjonal, europeisk og norsk klimarett mot 2030* (pp. 190–221). Universitetsforlaget.

Setzer, J., & Higham, C. (2022). Global trends in climate change litigation: 2022 Snapshot. Retrieved 11.05.2023 from https://www.lse.ac.uk/granthaminstitute/publication/global-trends-in-climate-change-litigation-2022/

Setzer, J., & Higham, C. (2023). Global trends in climate change litigation: 2023 Snapshot. Retrieved 24.04.2024 from https://www.lse.ac.uk/granthaminstitute/wp-content/uploads/2023/06/Global_trends_in_climate_change_litigation_2023_snapshot.pdf

Sjåfjell, B. (2023). Sustainability and law in the Anthropocene. In U. Münster, T. H. Eriksen, & S. A. Schoroer (Eds.), *Responding to the Anthropocene. Perspectives from twelve academic disciplines* (pp. 83–106). Scandinavian Academic Press.

Stortinget. (2018). The Constitution, as laid down on 17 May 1814 by the Constituent Assembly at Eidsvoll and subsequently amended, most recently in May 2018. Translation from the Storting. Retrieved 27.01.2021 from https://www.stortinget.no/globalassets/pdf/english/constitutionenglish.pdf

Supreme Court. (2020). Supreme Court judgement. Pronounced 22 December 2020. Case no.: HR-2020-2472-P (sak nr. 20-051052SIV-HRET). Retrieved 18.10.2023 from https://climatecasechart.com/wp-content/uploads/non-us-case-documents/2020/20201222_HR-2020-846-J_judgment.pdf

Takle, M. (2021). Solidarity with future generations? Protection clauses in constitution. In A. Falch-Eriksen, M. Takle, & B. Slagsvold (Eds.), *Generational tensions and solidarity within advanced welfare states* (pp. 59–72). Routledge.

Takle, M. (2023). Citizenship for future generations: The inclusion of future generations in welfare state considerations. In M. Takle, J. S. Vedeler, M. Schoyen, K. Klette-Bøhler, & A. Falch-Eriksen (Eds.), *Citizenship and social exclusion at the margins of the welfare state* (pp. 108–120). Routledge.

Tremmel, J. (Ed.) (2006). *Handbook of intergenerational justice*. Edward Elgar.

Tremmel, J. (2022). Generationsgerechtigkeit und Nachhaltigkeit. *Burger & Staat*, *3*, 203–209.

Urgenda Foundation. (2023). Landmark decision by Dutch Supreme Court. Retrieved 06.10.2023 from https://www.urgenda.nl/en/themas/climate-case/

Voigt, C. (2021). The first climate judgement before the Norwegian Supreme Court: Aligning law with politics. *Journal of Environmental Law*, *33*, 697–710.

Weiss, N. (2021). How to integrate environmental law into constitutional law: The German experience. *Justice climatique: perspectives des Île's de l'océan Indien*, *31*, 171–175.

Ytterstad, A., Houeland, C., & Jordhus-Lier, D. (2022). Heroes of the day after tomorrow: "The oil worker" in Norwegian climate coverage 2017–2021. *Journalism Practice*, *16*(2–3), 317–333.

8

ECONOMIC DEBT AND SAVINGS FOR FUTURE GENERATIONS

Introduction

Fiscal rules are one of the most binding forms of institutional constraints, justified by the need to consider future generations. This makes them suitable for examining the strengths and weaknesses of such bindings in practical politics. An increasing number of countries worldwide have adopted rules-based fiscal frameworks over the past two decades. There are different types of fiscal rules, but they aim to set rules for budget balance and limit expenses that affect public expenditure and debt. Countries introducing fiscal rules mostly do so for economic reasons, but there is also often an underlying social norm to prevent the transfer of debt to future generations or to ensure savings.

Like the other empirical chapters, this chapter raises three questions derived from the concept of solidarity with future generations, as discussed in Chapter 4. (i) What do the *commitments* by including financial constraints for future generations involve? (ii) How *binding* are these financial constraints for practical policy? (iii) What other societal concerns are in *tension* with the financial constraints followed by the fiscal rules for future generations?

Germany and Norway are analysed as examples of countries that have adopted fiscal rules and justified them with references to a concern for future generations. These countries are similar regarding the underlying social norm of considering future generations financially. Still, there are crucial differences between them. Germany has established a national fiscal debt brake in its Basic Law, imposing restrictions on how much money the country can borrow at both the federal and regional (*Länder*) levels. Norway has established a fiscal guideline defining the percentage the state can use as national budget expenditures of the Government Pension Fund Global, hereafter the

DOI: 10.4324/9781003400806-10
This chapter has been made available under a CC-BY-NC-ND 4.0 license.

Petroleum Fund. This was the name of the fund until 2006 and is still commonly used as the name of the fund.

The first section of this chapter presents an overview of the trend of countries that have adopted fiscal rules worldwide. Most documents used in this overview are retrieved from the International Monetary Fund (IMF) global debt database, which provides information on 190 countries categorised as advanced economies, emerging market economies, and low-income countries, dating back to 1950. Documents from the European Commission are also included. The second section analyses the German debt brake. The Germany study is based on the German Basic Law and documents from German Federal Constitutional Court, German *Bundestag*, German Federal Ministry of Finance and reports from the German Council of Economic Experts (*Sachverständigenrat*). The third section examines the Norwegian fiscal guideline within the framework of the Petroleum Fund. The Norwegian study includes Norwegian reports from government-appointed commissions, government white papers presented to parliament, and Acts the government presents to the parliament. The fourth section elaborates on what kinds of resources are passed on to future generations. Finally, the last section discusses how the financial constraints represent one-dimensional institutional constraints in a world threatened by environmental damages, where today's generations pass on serious problems to their descendants.

National fiscal rules

A fiscal rule is a long-standing constraint on fiscal policy through numerical limitations on a country's budget. Fiscal rules typically aim to correct distorted incentives and resist pressures for overspending, particularly in good times (IMF, 2022). A growing number of countries worldwide have adopted rules-based fiscal frameworks over the past two decades, and the increase has been particularly pronounced in Europe (Davoodi et al., 2022). While only around 10 countries had fiscal rules in the early 1990s, 105 countries had fiscal rules at the end of 2021 (IMF, 2022). While there are different types of fiscal rules, a typical trait is that they set an explicit ceiling for public debt, often expressed as a percentage of gross domestic product (GDP). The aim is to set rules for budget balance and limit expenses that affect public expenditure and debt. An increasing number of countries have improved the legal basis of their national fiscal rules, and many have also put formal enforcement mechanisms in place (Davoodi et al., 2022).

While advanced economies have been frontrunners in adopting fiscal rules, such rules have been increasingly common among emerging markets and developing economies since the late 2000s. By the end of 2021, there were more than twice as many emerging markets and developing economies with fiscal rules than advanced economies (IMF, 2022). This increase has been primarily driven by the adoption of rules in the aftermath of large shocks like financial crises. Emerging markets and developing economies are the groups of countries with the highest debt in the world. Over the past decades, fiscal deficits, and public debt ratios have increased enormously in many countries (IMF, 2022). The public debt ratio is the ratio of a country's public debt to GDP. The debt-to-GDP ratio reliably indicates a country's ability to pay back its debts.

Rules-based fiscal frameworks are vulnerable when countries are under pressure, such as during the COVID-19 pandemic. Many of the 105 countries in the IMF databases modified their fiscal rules in response to this crisis. While some countries activated an escape clause, others suspended the fiscal rules temporarily or modified the fiscal rule limits (Davoodi et al., 2022). These modifications show how fiscal rules can have considerable flexibility, and the COVID-19 pandemic led to a sharp rise in deficits and debt. About 90% of the 105 countries had deficits larger than their rule limits in 2020. Fiscal rules have not prevented a large and persistent debt build-up over time. On average, countries exceeded the deficit and debt limits during about 50% of the time during 2004–2021 (Davoodi et al., 2022).

In Europe, signing the Maastricht Treaty in 1992 led several countries to introduce fiscal rules. This was part of the establishment of the European Economic and Monetary Union. At the end of the 1990s, the member states agreed to lay down rules for budget monitoring under the EU's Stability and Growth Pact. These specified that the public deficit must be at most 3% of GDP, and public debt must not exceed 60% of GDP. In 2005, the criteria were maintained, but the decision to declare a country with an excessive deficit was based on additional parameters (European Commission, 2005).

As a result of the financial crisis of 2008, the member states signed a Fiscal Compact in 2012, stipulating that a structural deficit limit be adopted in national legislation as of 2013 (Bom, 2019). In Europe, new pressures on upholding fiscal rules came with the COVID-19 pandemic and Russia's invasion of Ukraine (European Commission, 2022). In most EU member states, the rules were suspended in 2020 but are planned to be reinstated in 2024. However, this raises a dilemma. While many European governments far exceed their deficit and debt limits, they must invest to combat climate change, and for this, most EU member states need to borrow money.

German debt brake rule

Germany has restrictions on how much money the country can borrow at both the federal and *Länder* levels. The consideration of future generations is crucial in the justification for these restrictions. The principle of balanced budgets is anchored in Article 109 of the Basic Law which states "The budgets of the Federation and the Länder shall, in principle, be balanced without revenue from credits" (Basic Law, Art. 109(3)). This article formulates the principle of the *Schuldenbremse*, or debt brake rule, adopted under a reform of the German federal system in 2009.

In addition, Article 115 of the Basic Law stipulates the basic structure of the debt brake and the method for calculating permissible net borrowing for the federal government. This limits Germany's structural net borrowing to 0.35% of GDP for new loans and thereby allows for adjustments that take cyclical factors into consideration, that means they allow for adjustments that take account of fluctuations in the economy. Such a "cyclical component" at the federal level implies that the debt brake provides for increased borrowing when economic development deviates from normal conditions.

The combination of these two articles in the Basic Law authorises the majority in the *Bundestag* to issue decisions allowing the federal government to suspend the debt brake in the event of natural catastrophes or unusual emergency situations that are beyond governmental control and are substantially harmful to the state's financial capacity (Basic Law, Art. 109(3); Art. 115(2)). We return to these options for exemptions for the federal government in the following, but first, we discuss how budget restraints have historically been included in German policy.

Fiscal rules with constitutional status have been restricting fiscal policy in Germany since long before the introduction of the debt brake. Both the 1871 constitution of the German Reich and the Weimar Constitution of 1919 restricted public borrowing (Burret et al., 2013). Also, the 1949 version of the Basic Law included a balanced budget rule. At that time, borrowing was excluded in principle and allowed only for exceptional needs and special purposes, but the exceptions were based on vague criteria for when and how this could be done (Burret, 2013).

A 1969 reform provided for a revised balanced budget rule. This reform introduced what is frequently called the "golden rule of fiscal policy." According to the German Federal Ministry of Finance (2022), the golden rule stated that the government may only increase new borrowing if, at the same time, its net assets increase by at least the same amount.

> The argument justifying this approach is that net government investment (= gross investment minus depreciation) is accompanied by asset formation on the government side, and that this benefits future generations, which means that it is fair for future generations to bear a share of the financing. Behind this lies the idea that productive public investments in themselves increase future potential GDP per inhabitant. The golden rule is designed to prevent the current generation from spending at the expense of future generations.
>
> *(Ministry of Finance, 2022, p. 21)*

Furthermore, the ministry states that the reform from 1969 was geared towards this golden rule, and exceptions were only allowed to avert a "disturbance of the general economic equilibrium." However, the government notes, the interpretation of the Basic Law diverged from the golden rule on critical points. Even grants and subsidies, which did not constitute assets for the government entity itself, were counted as gross investments (Ministry of Finance, 2022). This led to discussions about how to define investment and called for reforms to ensure restrictions on debt (Grohmann, 2013).

The German law reform in 2009

In 2009, there were reforms of the constitutional rules for budget restrictions, which led to what was referred to earlier as the debt brake. These changes received the required two-thirds majority in the *Bundestag* and *Bundesrat* (Bundestag, 2009). Generally, there were three reasons why such reforms were perceived as necessary.

Firstly, the institutional and economic prerequisites for fiscal and economic policy changed significantly when the EU established the Economic and Monetary Union in 2002, as discussed earlier. We should add that Germany has been a driving force in establishing these European framework conditions, and, in this context, Germany's economic strength matters. German fiscal choices set the tone for euro area as a whole, as the country accounts for almost 30% of the euro area economy (Vallee et al., 2021).

Secondly, since the 1970s, there has been a trend in Germany for increasing public debt as a percentage of GDP. Some reasons for this increase were exceptional events such as the oil price crises in the 1970s and German reunification in 1990. There was a particularly sharp rise following the 2008/2009 financial crisis, and the debt reached a peak of 82.0% of GDP in 2010 (Ministry of Finance, 2022). Since 2010, the public debt has only partially been reduced (German Council of Economic Experts, 2019).

Thirdly, the federal and *Länder* governments are autonomous and independent of one another in the management of their respective budgets. Several of the *Länder* had borrowed in large amounts, and there was a need for coordination (Grohmann, 2013). The changes were adopted under a reform of the German federal system and applied both to the federation and the *Länder*. The reform entailed stricter conditions for borrowing for the *Länder* than for the federal government. A transition period initially applied for the federal government between 2011 and 2016, during which the rules were gradually tightened, and the transition period for the *Länder* remained in force until 2020.

The government's legislative proposal, which was passed, highlighted the importance of concern for future generations (Bundestag, 2009). According to the government an adjustment of the intergenerational distribution of burden was necessary. The reason was the country's high level of national debt. The previous legislation had allowed for credit financing of (gross) investments and would therefore be replaced.

> With a view to intergenerational equity, structural debt should be possible to a very limited extent within the framework of the new principle. The budgetary legislature's leeway will be expanded, particularly for measures that will benefit future generations by permanently strengthening growth and sustainable development. By granting a very limited structural scope for debt, there is by no means an automatic intention that this should always be exploited in ongoing budget planning.
>
> *(Bundestag, 2009, p. 6, my translation)*

The idea of considering future generations in the form of indirect reciprocity is fundamental for the debt brake. Refraining from handing over debt to coming generations is a fundamental premise and commitment in German political discussion. There is, however, no consensus on this idea. In 2009, the Green Party and the Left Party voted against, while the Liberal Party abstained from voting. With the support of the Social Democrats and the Conservatives, the agreement achieved the required two-thirds majority in the *Bundestag* and *Bundesrat*. A decisive question, however, is to what extent and how these commitments enshrined in the Basic Law are binding in practice.

Exceptions from the German debt brake

Main reforms of the debt brake imply a constitutional reform, and this requires a two-thirds majority in the *Bundestag* and *Bundesrat*. This implies strong institutional constraints. However, the debt brake can be circumvented in other ways; as we have seen earlier, the debt brake allows for exceptions. The exceptions apply in the case of natural disasters and unusual emergency situations that are beyond the authorities' control and have a major negative impact on public finances (Basic Law, Art. 109(3); Art. 115(2)). A simple majority in the *Bundestag* is required to meet such exceptional situations with increased credits.

The COVID-19 pandemic was such an exceptional situation, and the exception rule was applied for the 2020 and 2021 federal budgets. Special-purpose funds (*Sondervermögen*) were established, and an individual repayment plan was prepared for each of the years with budget overruns. Accordingly, the amounts borrowed in 2020 and 2021 must be repaid according to a repayment plan (Bundestag, 2020; 2022a).

As a direct response to the Russian invasion of Ukraine, the government established a 100-billion-euro Defence Fund in 2022, to strengthen the alliance and German defence capability (Bundestag, 2022b). This fund was created as a special-purpose fund, which lies alongside and in addition to the ordinary defence budget. Although the fund was created as an exception to the ordinary budget, it was not implemented within the framework of the debt brake in line with the exception rules applied for the COVID-19 funds.

Instead, new exemption legislation was introduced. The required two-thirds majority in the *Bundestag* amended Article 87a of the constitution in which the new paragraph 1a states "For the purpose of strengthening its ability to honour its alliance obligations and its defence capability, the Federation may establish a special trust with its own credit authorisation for a single amount of up to 100 billion euros..." (Basic Law, 2022). This shows that a severe security policy situation leads to new exceptions.

Germany has several special-purpose funds, which represent an additional budget for financing specific, defined tasks. The revenues for a special-purpose fund come from the regular federal budget or legally specified exceptions from the debt brake as the COVID-19 fund or by establishing a new special-purpose fund like the defence fund. As of 2023, the federal government has a total of 29 special-purpose funds, and the importance of such funds has increased in recent years (German Council of Economic Experts, 2023).

In 2022, the German Bundestag allocated 200 billion euros to a Climate and Transformation Fund to finance measures to achieve the federal government's climate protection goals, particularly to decarbonise the economy and international climate protection. This fund has revenues from various sources. Interesting in this regard is that the *Bundestag* passed a law that provided for transferring 60 billion euros borrowed as a part of the COVID-19 fund from 2021 (Bundestag, 2022a). The COVID-19 fund was created as an exception to the debt brake, but these euros had not been used in response to the pandemic. The government, therefore, wanted to use them as a part of the Climate and Transformation Fund in subsequent financial years. The transfer was carried out retroactively in 2022 for the then-ended budget year 2021 (Bundestag, 2022a).

Members of the CDU/CSU *Bundestag* parliamentary group who voted against the law, appealed the case to the German Federal Constitutional Court. The court concluded that this act is incompatible with the Basic Law and is void (Constitutional Court, 2023). It argued that the law does not satisfy the constitutional requirements for emergency borrowing. The reason was that the *Bundestag* had not sufficiently demonstrated the necessary factual connection between the emergency and the crisis management measures taken in response. They had neither followed the principle of annual budgeting nor the rule that the budget must be determined in advance (Constitutional Court, 2023). The court's decision meant that the Climate and Transformation Fund must be reduced by 60 billion euros and the government had to find other financial sources.

This Constitutional Court's decision shows that the debt brake involves strict, binding restrictions on the German budget discipline. Like the court's previous decision in the climate lawsuit, it protects future generations. Both judgements apply the principle that current generations should not live at the expense of the future. As far as the debt brake is concerned, applying such a principle presupposes that saving does not come at the expense of necessary investments today to secure future infrastructure.

However, the exceptions with the COVID-19 funds and the Defence Fund reveal that it is possible to circumvent the restrictions. This means that the debt brake only involves binding budgetary discipline until something out of the ordinary happens, and the *Bundestag* allows exceptions for borrowing new expenses beyond the ordinary budgets. The prerequisites are that the reasons must have substance and be in line with the Basic Law. COVID-19 was defined as such an exception from the debt brake, while the Russian invasion of Ukraine led to new amendments of the Basic Law.

However, the majority in the *Bundestag* emphasised that even if Germany borrowed to create special funds, the country would stick to the debt brake for the sake of future generations. In connection with the Defence Fund, the majority, for example, acknowledged: "It remains the case that the federal government's debt must be kept within the limits set by the Basic Law in the interest of intergenerational equity" (Bundestag, 2022b, p. 8, my translation).

Tensions between debts and investments in Germany

Maintaining binding fiscal policy rules for future generations is in tension with loan-financed investments. The idea that today's generations should not pass financial burdens onto their descendants must be weighed against the fact that debt-based investments may be necessary to hand over a sustainable society to the people of the future. A fiscal policy that is too tight could prevent investments that are necessary to maintain societal structures. Moreover, by not allowing for debt-financed investments in material infrastructure the costs of permanent public investment fall exclusively on current generations, while future generations also receive the benefits (Bom, 2019).

With the aim to find solutions to these tensions between debt and investments, the idea of a "golden rule of fiscal policy" has been discussed at European level (European Commission, 2022). The golden rule allows for loan-based financing of material investments that benefit future generations, while the fiscal rule applies to all other types of public spending (Bom, 2019). This is a way of distributing the costs of material investments between generations and, at the same time, ensuring that current generations do not consume and transfer the costs to their descendants (European Commission, 2022). The golden rule of fiscal policy aims to even out wealth across time and generations.

In Germany, we have seen that these trade-offs were historically regulated by the golden rule of fiscal policy, but that this led to discussions about how to define investment (Grohmann, 2013; Ministry of Finance, 2022). The revised version of the debt brake from 2009 took this partly into account. While it has not defined what investments mean, the cyclical component and the exceptions rules give fiscal policy a certain degree of flexibility in terms of investments (Feld et al., 2020).

New investments in Germany are required. This was the main conclusion in the annual report for 2023/2024 from the German Council of Economic Experts. This Council is an independent academic body set up by law and mandated to provide an impartial expert view on periodic assessments of macroeconomic developments in Germany. It argued that Germany's medium-term growth prospects are at a historic low. According to the medium-term projection of the Council, "potential output will only grow by an average of 0.4 per cent per year until 2028 if current dynamics continue unchanged" (German Council of Economic Experts, 2023).

There are voices in Germany, but also outside the country, calling for higher borrowing in Germany and reform or the abolition of the debt brake. The most straightforward argument is that the debt brake has considerably weakened the country's ability to act in the face of crisis, modernise its economy, and allow for an effective climate and energy transition (Fratzscher, 2023; Vallee et al., 2021). Debt provides opportunities for new investments, which can increase the incomes of future generations, and prevent conflicts and disasters when, among other things, infrastructure is not maintained. Accordingly, the debt brake in its current form does not reflect the interests of the future generation (Breuer, 2021).

Another more fundamental argument is that fiscal policy should be subordinated to other societal objectives. Consequently, the main problem with the debt brake is the current focus on stabilising the debt-to-GDP ratio rather than solving the country's main challenges. To handle challenges like decarbonisation, demographic change, and the long-term stabilisation of the external balance with other countries, "deficit and debt would be the dependent, subordinated variables that would have to adjust" (Sigl-Glöckner et al., 2021, p. 27).

Both types of arguments show that a broader discussion beyond the purely economic framework regarding commitments for future generations is necessary. In a world threatened by environmental damage and where there is a great need to invest in environmental measures, it is appropriate to discuss which resources are transferred between generations.

Norwegian Petroleum Fund and fiscal guideline

Like Germany, Norway has binding budget restrictions, which are justified by considering future generations. In contrast to Germany, these are not restrictions on how much debt the country may have. They are restrictions on the percentage of the country's Petroleum Fund the state can use as national budget expenditures. Since 2006, the fund's formal name is Government Pension Fund Global, but it is commonly called *Oljefondet*, i.e. the Petroleum Fund.

In 1990, the government established the state-owned Petroleum Fund of Norway and has regularly transferred capital from oil revenues to this fund. In March 2024, the fund's market value is NOK 17,448 billion, equivalent to more than 1.6 billion US dollars (NBIM, 2024a). Decisive for the Norwegian budget restrictions is that parts of the Petroleum Fund are used to cover expenditures in the national budget. In 2024, Fund spending covers more than 20% of fiscal budget expenditure, and this share has doubled since 2012 (Meld. St. 1 (2023–2024)). These revenues are of great importance for Norwegian welfare and give reasons to consider the petroleum fund a political success (Øvald et al., 2019).

The budget restrictions are laid down in the fiscal guideline (*handlingsregelen*), which was introduced in 2001 (St. Meld. 29 (2000–2001)). It says that the use of the Petroleum Fund for national budget expenses must, over time, be in line with the expected real return on the fund. This was estimated at 4% of the fund until 2017, when it was reduced to 3%. The argument for introducing this guideline was to separate the revenues from petroleum production from welfare provisions (St. Meld. 29 (2000–2001)). The aim was to prevent an overheated economy by phasing petroleum revenues gradually into the Norwegian economy and redistributing the capital over several years (St. Meld. 29 (2000–2001)). As the average return has been higher than 3% and the Norwegian state has transferred income to the fund each year, it has gradually increased in value.

As the income from petroleum production increased, the pressure to increase the use of funds for welfare provisions became stronger. As Lie (2015) argues, with the fiscal guideline, the politicians presented savings for future generations as a good purpose that could contend with all other good purposes competing for attention and support. Lie (2015) sees this as a moral appeal that is understandable and is also in harmony with challenges and discussions about other long-term societal challenges (Lie, 2015, p. 235). By introducing the fiscal guideline, petroleum production would not lead to increased spending in the state budget, and thereby lead to instability in the Norwegian economy. The fiscal guideline had a simplicity and a moral anchor linked to the concerns for future generations.

This is confirmed in a government white paper published two decades after introducing the fiscal guideline. It states that during the two decades the fiscal guideline has been in effect, it has proposed that the fund's capital be used to provide a fair distribution between generations and facilitate a stable development in the Norwegian economy (Meld. St. 1 (2023–2024)).

The reasons for implementing the fiscal guideline show commitment to future generations. The idea is that the nation's wealth should be shared fairly between generations. This is equivalent to an idea of indirect reciprocity. Examining the establishment of the Petroleum Fund is necessary to discuss in more detail what these commitments involve. It is important to see the fund and the fiscal guideline in the context of which activities generate income for the fund and what significance this will have for future people.

The establishment of the Norwegian Petroleum Fund

Since Phillips Petroleum first found oil in the Norwegian sector of the North Sea in 1969, Norwegian politicians have ensured the state gathers a large part of the income from petroleum production. At the turn of the 1970s, when Norwegian oil production was beginning, Norway was economically an average country in the industrialised world in terms of the Organisation for Economic Co-operation and Development (OECD) measures (Schiefloe, 2016). The politicians' aim of keeping national control over petroleum production was based on the idea that natural resources belong to the people (Lie, 2012, pp. 143–146).

A parliamentary report from 1974 that laid the foundation for Norwegian petroleum production repeated this position on common property rights several times (St. Meld. 25 (1973–1974)). In the 1970s, there was a political consensus that Norway should adhere to a moderate pace of extraction of petroleum resources (Lie et al., 2016). There were no explicit references to sustainable development, but the entire report was characterised by a perspective that emphasised the need to take environmental considerations into account when oil extraction was discussed.

In 1984, a parliamentary report introduced a national wealth model to evaluate the use of petroleum resources (St. Meld. 32 (1984–1985)). The report operationalised this wealth in terms of four forms of capital: natural capital, human capital, fixed real capital, and financial capital. All these four forms of capital could be converted into a monetary equivalent, and the model assumes substitutability between different forms of capital (St. Meld. 32 (1984–1985)).

By applying the national wealth model, politicians introduced simultaneously an understanding of petroleum reserves that can best be described in terms of weak sustainability. This means that natural capital and other types of capital (in this case mainly human-made capital) are substitutable. This requires all forms of capital to be converted into an equivalent value, with money serving as a universal measure for valuation. A common unit of measurement is seen as useful to gauge the relative importance of natural resources in relation to other goods and services (O'Neill, 2017). Sustainable development (in the weak meaning) is achieved when the total value of the aggregate stock of capital is maintained, or ideally increased, for future generations. Accordingly, the politicians used the metaphorical conversion of non-renewable resources to financial wealth.

> If annual consumption of petroleum revenues is lower than annual income, some of the revenues may be invested in other property assets. One will then over time build up other forms of wealth. This wealth could be regarded as a conversion of the petroleum wealth. Such a wealth will, when the period of oil extraction is over, provide a basis for taking advantage of petroleum revenues in the future.
>
> *(St. Meld. 32 (1984–1985), p. 74, my own translation)*

The national wealth model made it possible to measure how one could offset a decrease in natural resources by an adequate increase in financial capital. The current generation's responsibility towards future generations consists of providing that the following generations have at least as much natural or human-made capital at its disposal as itself.

This weak sustainability should be seen in contrast to strong sustainability, which is based on the idea that there is a qualitative difference between natural capital and human-made capital and substitutability is strictly limited. The consumption of non-renewable natural capital is irreversible, and one cannot be sure of the effects for future generations due to destruction of the environment (Habib, 2013). Moreover, human-made capital requires natural capital for its production and can thus never be a complete substitute for natural capital (Gough, 2017). Strong sustainability implies that what constitutes the current generation's responsibility towards future generations is to conserve the irreplaceable stocks of critical natural capital. Accordingly, the policy would include that it might be crucial for future generations to have access to non-renewable petroleum wealth.

When the government established the Petroleum Fund in 1990, it applied the national wealth model based on weak sustainability. The argument was that the transfer of revenues from petroleum production to a petroleum fund would prevent the decline of petroleum reserves reducing Norwegians' common national wealth (Ot. Prp. 29 (1989–1990)). The Norwegian Government Petroleum Fund Act formulated the purpose of the fund as pursuing long-term considerations by using petroleum revenues. Balancing current spending with long-term interests was based on an institutionalising of self-restraints (Øvald et al., 2019). The financial capital in the fund could not be used for consumption without a decision in parliament. This was specified through the fiscal guideline in 2001, as introduced earlier. The arguments were formulated in economic terms and a concept of weak sustainability.

> The Petroleum Fund is based on extraction and sale of a non-renewable natural resource. Through the Petroleum Fund it is possible to build up an

> alternative wealth that can provide a return over a longer period, and from which future generations can benefit.
>
> *(St. Meld. 29 (2000–2001), p. 4, my translation)*

This long-term idea for the Petroleum Fund is expressed, among other things, by how the *Storting* renamed the fund in 2006 to the Government Pension Fund Global (Ot. Prp. 2 (2005–2006)). There were no political decisions concerning whether and when the fund should be used to cover future pension costs (Innst. S. 195 (2004–2005)). The politicians' idea behind the renaming seems rather to have been to send a message to the population that they had long-term goals for the use of petroleum revenues.

In the government's reports to the *Storting*, we can read that oil revenues represent a non-renewable natural resource, and savings in the fund aim to distribute this resource across time and generations (Meld. St. 26 (2016–2017), p. 113). The Norwegian Bank Investment Management (NBIM), which has been responsible for the management of the fund since the late 1990s, describes the fund's aim on its webpage "to ensure responsible and long-term management of revenue from Norway's oil and gas resources, so that this wealth benefits both current and future generations" (NBIM, 2024a).

Both the Petroleum Fund and the fiscal guideline are justified based on consideration for future generations. These commitments involve the state extracting oil and gas, selling it abroad, and depositing the income in the fund. At the same time, the state established a fiscal guideline to ensure that the current generation does not empty the North Sea of oil and gas and use all the proceeds from the sale without transferring anything to future Norwegian generations.

From a national perspective, Norway shows an admirable ability to administer a common good so that natural resources benefit the entire Norwegian population. This is shown by comparing how Norway and the United Kingdom have had different approaches to managing offshore hydrocarbon resources in the North Sea. While both countries produced similar amounts of hydrocarbons, the Norwegian state earned almost two and a half times more revenues than the United Kingdom from 1971 to 2011 (Jamasb & Sen, 2022). While both countries derived their revenue from taxes and fees, Norway also had revenues from the State's Direct Financial Interests, and dividends from the participation of state-owned petroleum companies (Jamasb & Sen, 2022).

From a cosmopolitan perspective, this is a narrow and nation-oriented policy. Seen from this perspective the surplus should be distributed to the world's poorest people today, and not future rich Norwegians, or alternatively, natural resources should be preserved to reduce greenhouse gas emissions worldwide (Finneron-Burns, forthcoming; Wilson & Hessen, 2014).

Petroleum Fund's role in the current Norwegian economy

Macroeconomic indicators for the petroleum sector show that this sector contributes 26% of the Norwegian GDP, 42% of the State's revenues, 17% of the country's total investments and 54% of the total exports. In these figures, the service and supplier industry are not included (Norwegian Petroleum, 2023). As mentioned in Chapter 1, Norway's oil production covers about 2% of the global demand, and its natural gas production covers approximately 3%. Norway supplies between 20% and 25% of the EU and United Kingdom's gas demand (Norwegian Petroleum, 2024). These figures show that the petroleum sector is of considerable importance to the Norwegian economy.

The Norwegian Petroleum Fund consists of four types of revenues the state receives from petroleum production. Firstly, this income includes tax from the oil companies, which is composed of an ordinary company taxation of 24% plus a special tax of 54%. Secondly, there is an income from the State's Direct Financial Interest, known as Petoro since 2001, which is a system under which the state owns holdings in several oil and gas fields, pipelines, and onshore facilities. Thirdly, there are revenues from direct state ownership in Statoil, known as Equinor since May 2018, in which the state owns 67% of shares. Finally, there are area fees and environmental taxes (Norwegian Petroleum, 2023).

The Sovereign Wealth Fund Institute (2023a) ranks the Norwegian Petroleum Fund as the world's largest wealth fund, followed by similar funds in China, Abu Dhabi, Kuwait, and Saudi Arabia. The distinctive aspect of sovereign wealth funds that sets them apart from other vehicles of investment is their state ownership. This means they have a longer-term horizon for their investments than other investors, and they have broader social welfare objectives, rather than solely maximisation of financial returns (Bolton et al., 2012; Lansley, 2016). As mentioned in Chapter 1, the Norwegian fund is the largest single owner in the world's stock markets, owning almost 1.5% of all shares in the world's listed companies (NBIM, 2024b). According to the Sovereign Wealth Fund Institute (2023b), around 40 sovereign wealth funds have been created since 2005. Most countries with sovereign wealth funds are resource-rich countries with mainly oil as their natural resource.

In contrast to how the German debt brake is anchored in the Basic Law, the Norwegian fiscal guideline is implemented in the Norwegian Government Petroleum Fund Act. Only a simple majority decision in the *Storting* is required to change it. In other words, the guideline is not strikingly binding on Norwegian politicians. However, the fiscal guideline was very soon accepted by all political parties and the Norwegian public (Lie, 2015). This is probably decisive for budget restrictions to have proven binding in practice. Since the fiscal guideline was established, all Norwegian national budgets have stayed within its framework. The national budget for 2024 emphasised:

> The fiscal guideline calls for the fund capital to be spent to provide a fair distribution between generations and facilitate stable development in the Norwegian economy. These considerations need to be weighed against one another when assessing fund spending.
>
> *(Meld. St. 1 (2023–2024), p. 52, my translation)*

As we have seen, the fund's market value has increased considerably over the past 20 years, from around NOK 2,000 billion in 2007 to around NOK 17,448 billion 2024, equivalent to more than 1.6 billion US dollars in March 2024 (NBIM, 2024a). Simultaneously, the fund's share of fiscal budget expenditure has doubled from 2012 to 2024, and in 2024 this share covers more than 20% (Meld. St. 1 (2023–2024)). This means that even using a tiny share of 3% of the fund, which is the fund's expected real return, implies crucial national dependence on the fund. Still, the Norwegian budget restrictions require that the country continues to produce oil and gas even though as of 2016, the return from the Petroleum Fund exceeded current petroleum revenues for the first time (NOU 2017: 13, p. 93).

Ethical guidelines for Norwegian investments

There are tensions in Norway regarding whether investments in environmentally friendly projects can compensate for the environmental degradation caused by petroleum activity. The *Storting* decided on ethical guidelines for the management of the fund in 2004 (St. Meld. 2 (2003–2004). Accordingly, the fund should not make investments which result in unethical acts or omissions such as violations of basic humanitarian principles, gross human rights violations, gross corruption, or serious environmental degradation. With these ethical guidelines, investments should take environmental, economic, and social considerations into account (St. Meld. 2 (2003–2004)). In addition, a Council on Ethics for the fund has been established to evaluate whether the fund's investment in specified companies is inconsistent with its Ethical Guidelines (Norwegian Council on Ethics for GPFG, 2023).

In line with recommendations provided by the Ministry of Finance and the Council on Ethics appointed by the ministry, the Norwegian Bank Investment Management (NBIM) is responsible for the investments. NBIM defines its mission as "to safeguard and build financial wealth for future generations" (NBIM, 2024a). Moreover, it is a global investor with minority ownership in more than 9,000 companies in 73 countries. NBIM performs annual assessments in which it gathers information and analysis in three focus areas: children's rights, climate change, and water management

(NBIM, 2024a). With the aim of making the government's wealth less vulnerable to a permanent drop in oil and gas prices, NBIM (2017) recommended the removal of oil stocks from the benchmark index of the fund in 2017. In March 2019, the government followed this advice.

However, it is important to note that the ethical guidelines are applied after petroleum production is fulfilled. The question is thereby not whether to extract the petroleum, but rather how to invest the income from petroleum activity (Graver, 2004). The ethical investments can never fully compensate for the environmental consequences of the extraction of oil and gas. Accordingly, financial compensation cannot compensate for the environmental damages that are passed on to future generations by the combustion of oil and gas. While financial savings are made on grounds of indirect reciprocity with future generations, environmental damages cannot be compensated in the form of capital investments.

Financial savings and conservation of Norwegian nature

There is a more fundamental tension between financial savings and nature conservation. This tension is hardly expressed in connection with the Petroleum Fund. The opposition to oil and gas production is expressed in connection with the climate lawsuit, which we have seen in Chapter 7.

We have seen that in Norway, the idea that the current generation should not empty the North Sea of oil and gas without saving something for future generations has been a politically established norm since the 1970s. This responsibility is constituted by the idea that natural resources belong to the people, both current and future Norwegians. Over time, the understanding of how to save has changed. The idea of weak sustainability has increasingly come to dominate the argumentation in public documents dealing with the Petroleum Fund. This has helped to create a distinction between oil and gas production on the one hand and the use of the income on the other.

In 2016, the government devoted an entire chapter in a parliamentary report to explaining how the national wealth model is applied to investments in the fund (Meld. St. 26 (2016–2017)). According to the government, national wealth can be calculated in different ways, but it is generally defined as the net present value of the future consumption opportunities it provides. The government includes calculations for four components. Firstly, human capital is estimated as the net present value of future labour input. Secondly, natural resources are petroleum wealth, which is calculated as the net present value of future economic profit in the petroleum sector. As a simplification, the government notes that other natural resources are disregarded. Thirdly, fixed assets are the estimated value calculated at the replacement cost of such assets. Fourthly, financial wealth is the country's net financial wealth abroad (Meld. St. 26 (2016–2017)).

This national wealth model has over time become important for understanding the Petroleum Fund as savings for future generations. According to this model, oil and gas are natural capital that can be converted into other types of capital, in this case financial wealth.

> The inflow of capital to the GPFG is largely a conversion of oil and gas resources on the Norwegian continental shelf into foreign financial assets. This conversion separates the net petroleum revenues from the state's other income.
>
> *(Meld. St. 26 (2016–2017), p. 18)*

The idea is that the Norwegian state's use of non-renewable natural capital is sustainable as long as the financial assets abroad are augmented accordingly. When politicians present the Petroleum Fund as savings for future generations, it is framed as a moral act of extracting oil and gas in the North Sea to save financial investments abroad for future generations. In this frame, the reduction of non-renewable fossil fuels is described as something good as it is seen as a way of raising future welfare. While there are some vague speculations of what future generations will prefer, there is no discussion of their need for functional ecological systems. Saving of financial capital is seen as a compensation for the depletion of non-renewable fossil fuels, rather than defining specific characteristics required of an intergenerational compensation (Spash, 2002).

Although the government has a long-term perspective for the petroleum fund, there is no guarantee that the fund will ensure future welfare. This approach to sustainability leaves out important discussions about compensation for harm to the environment caused by the use of fossil fuels (Spash, 2002). Furthermore, it overlooks what is emphasised in terms of strong sustainability that a minimum compensation for depletion of fossil fuels or damages made to the environment would require ecological systems to be maintained in such a way that future generations can meet their needs (Gough, 2017). In this perspective, it is possible that future Norwegian generations will prefer to have oil and gas on the seabed rather than a financial Petroleum Fund to cover payment of pensions.

What resources are passed on to future generations?

Germany and Norway are examples of a growing number of countries worldwide that have adopted rules-based fiscal frameworks over the past two decades. Germany has established a national fiscal debt brake in its Basic Law, which implies restrictions on how much money the country can borrow at both the federal and *Länder* levels. Norway has established a fiscal guideline defining the percentage the state can use as national budget expenditures of the Petroleum Fund. There are many financial reasons to introduce fiscal rules, and in addition to these Germany and Norway have justified their fiscal rules with references to future generations.

These two examples show the goals of preventing countries from transferring debt and ensuring savings for future generations. The commitments to such goals and the implementation of them can be analysed in terms of Rawls' (1971; 2001) proposal for a principle of "just savings." As discussed in Chapter 4, Rawls proposed a threshold to define current generations' obligations towards future generations. He argued that justice does not require people to save for future people. His main point was that current generations should do what is necessary to allow future people to live under just institutions (Rawls, 2001). However, as also discussed in Chapter 4, many later discussions have been reactions to Rawls' contribution, and the most fundamental criticism is that he was concerned with how much a generation should save and overlooked the question of what to save (Caney, 2018; Tremmel, 2009).

A one-dimensional approach to financial considerations has important weaknesses. It loses sight of other societal concerns, which are unsustainable in a world threatened by climate crises and reduced biodiversity. With today's environmental destruction, it is necessary to include a broader analysis of what resources are transferred from current to future generations, not just how much. It is essential to analyse which resources are transferred to future generations: financial debt, savings, or natural resources.

Graeber (2011) has studied the history of debt to ask the question of what human beings and human society actually owe one another. He discusses the relationship between moral obligations and debts and argues that these are often interwoven, and both are based on a language shaped by financial markets. On one level, Graeber argues, the difference between them is obvious.

> A debt is the obligation to pay a certain sum of money. As a result, a debt, unlike any other form of obligation can be precisely quantified. This allows debts to become simple, cold, and impersonal – which in turn, allows them to be transferable.
>
> *(Graeber, 2011, p. 13)*

Graeber distinguishes the obligation to pay a certain sum of money from owing a person a favour, which is owed to a person specifically and cannot easily be transferred. He has an anthropological approach where he emphasises the close connection between social ties and the transmission of values. Regarding money, Graeber argues, one only needs to calculate principal, balances, and rates of interest.

Accordingly, when the relationship between generations is turned into fiscal rules calculated in money, the relationships become impersonal, can be calculated, and they can be exchanged. If we are to examine fiscal rules from the perspective of intergenerational social solidarity, we need a broader approach where we also include social norms. In Germany and Norway, the justifications of the budget restrictions are based on ideas of indirect reciprocity in which future generations are framed as part of a community where they get their share of financial capital. This framing is based on a one-dimensional economic understanding that overlooks the consequences for nature.

Market-based instrumental nature values form the basis for today's policymaking. This is a crucial conclusion from the Intergovernmental Science-Policy Platform on Biodiversity and Ecosystem Services (IPBES). In the *Assessment Report on the Diverse Values and Valuation of Nature*, IPBES show that there is a dominant global focus on short-term profits and economic growth. This often excludes the consideration of multiple values of nature in policy decisions (IPBES, 2022). Moreover, it concludes:

> The way nature is valued in political and economic decisions is both a key driver of the global biodiversity crisis and a vital opportunity to address it, according to a four-year methodological assessment by 82 top scientists and experts from every region of the world.
>
> *(IPBES, 2022)*

This report, approved by representatives of the 139 member states, finds that economic and political decisions have predominantly prioritised certain values of nature, particularly market-based instrumental values of nature. Moreover, it argues that these market values, often privileged in policymaking, do not adequately reflect how changes in nature affect people's quality of life. One of the key messages to policy makers is:

> Despite the diversity of nature's values, most policymaking approaches have prioritized a narrow set of values at the expense of both nature and society, as well as of future generations, and have often ignored values associated with indigenous peoples' and local communities' world-views.
>
> *(IPBES, 2022, p. 10)*

By applying this evidence, Pascual et al. (2023) published an article in *Nature* in which they argue that a better understanding of how and why nature is undervalued is more urgent than ever. The authors propose a combination of values-centred approaches to improve valuation. They propose changes towards fairer treatment of people and nature, including intergenerational equity and sustainable futures. Such considerations are essential to decide what today's generations should pass on to their descendants and what opportunities future generations should have to shape their own lives.

One-dimensional institutional constraints

While the German goal is to prevent the state from leaving financial debt to future generations, the Norwegian goal is to ensure financial savings for future generations. Both country cases involve commitments with considerable institutional constraints on state budgets. These constraints are more comprehensive and binding in practice than the political and legal bindings discussed in previous chapters. This shows the strength of implementing financial commitments in practical politics. Moreover, it shows that substantial institutional bindings are possible.

In both countries, we find ideas that can be interpreted as indirect reciprocity between generations. In the German Bundestag, the debt brake is presented as commitments that will benefit future generations by permanently strengthening growth and sustainable development. In the Norwegian *Storting*, the Petroleum Fund and the fiscal guideline are presented as savings for future generations. The Norwegian commitments require the state to extract oil and gas, deposit the income in the fund, and establish a fiscal guideline to ensure that the current generation transfers part of the income to future Norwegians.

The fiscal rules involve not only commitments but also significant institutional constraints in both countries. The German budget restrictions can only be changed through a constitutional reform. The judgement from the German Federal Constitutional Court in 2023 confirmed this strict German budget discipline. However, the debt brake can be circumvented. This possibility has been used in recent years, such as with COVID-19 and with Russia's invasion of Ukraine. These exceptions show crises in the present which create obstacles for a long-term policy. Today's concern for future people seems most manageable in good times.

The Norwegian budget restrictions are designed as guidelines with weak formal bindings. A simple majority decision in the *Storting* is required to change them. Nevertheless, the budget restrictions have proved binding in practice. One reason is that the fund's market value has increased significantly over the past 20 years, and using a small share of 3% of the fund has few consequences for the fund. At the same time, this use of the fund in the national budget means that around 20% of the expenditure comes from the Petroleum Fund.

The German debt brake and the Norwegian fiscal guideline involve specific goals which can be measured. These precise measurements make it possible to check whether the restrictions are complied with. The target for the German debt brake is precisely measured in the debt-to-GDP ratio every year. In Norway, the fiscal guideline is a precise target measured in a percentage of the fund size. However, the budget restrictions are one dimensional. In a world where today's generations pass on serious environmental problems to their descendants, the arguments about preventing debt or securing savings for future generations should be seen in a larger context of what resources are transferred to future generations.

In Germany and Norway, the budget restrictions lead to tensions with other societal concerns. Both have committed to an active environmental and resource policy and justified central policies by referring to a concern for future generations. They differ in the political context in which these policies are justified, and the economy is an important underlying factor. As discussed in Chapter 1, the German dilemma between the urgent need to consider secure alternative energy supplies since the Russian invasion in Ukraine in February 2022, and the need for long-term thinking to safeguard a healthy environment for future generations. The Norwegian paradox is that the country is taking a global lead in solving environmental challenges, while it simultaneously has large parts of its income from its petroleum activities.

In Germany, there are tensions between strict budget discipline and the need to borrow money for new investments. One argument against the debt brake is that budgets which are too tight prevent investments necessary to maintain societal structures. Debt provides opportunities for new investments, which can increase income for future generations. Another argument is that fiscal policy should be subordinated to other societal objectives. Accordingly, the main problem with the debt brake is that the current focus is on stabilising the debt-to-GDP ratio rather than solving the country's main challenge, which is to ensure the transition to renewable energy.

In Norway, there are tensions regarding which ethical considerations the Petroleum Fund takes in its investments. Another more fundamental tension concerns the large oil and gas sector, on which the petroleum fund's income is based. In public documents from the government and the *Storting*, the Petroleum Fund is framed in terms of weak sustainability. This implies that oil and gas as natural capital are converted into other types of capital, as in this case, financial investments. From this perspective, the current generation's responsibility towards future generations is to ensure that future generations have at least as much natural or human-made capital at their disposal as itself. This conversion of natural resources to money makes budget restrictions important. There are no considerations about whether future Norwegian generations might prefer oil and gas under the seabed rather than financial investments.

Summary

- A growing number of countries worldwide have adopted rules-based fiscal frameworks over the past two decades, and 105 countries had fiscal rules at the beginning of the 2020s.
- Germany and Norway have adopted fiscal rules and also justified them with references to a concern for future generations. The German case is about preventing debt, and the Norwegian case is about financial savings.

- Germany has established a national fiscal debt brake in its Basic Law, which establishes restrictions on how much money the country can borrow at both the federal and *Länder* levels.
- The German budget restrictions aim to ensure that current generations do not transfer debt to their descendants, and this can be interpreted in terms of an idea of indirect reciprocity.
- Norway has established a fiscal guideline defining the percentage the state can use as national budget expenditures of the Petroleum Fund.
- The fiscal guideline and the Petroleum Fund mean the state extracts oil and gas, deposits the income in the fund, and establishes a fiscal guideline to ensure that the current generation transfers part of the income to future Norwegians.
- German budget restrictions are binding as they can only be changed through a constitutional reform, but these bindings can be circumvented as the debt brake allows for exceptions such as the COVID-19 pandemic and Russia's invasion of Ukraine.
- Norwegian budget restrictions are designed as guidelines with weak bindings on the finances, but they have proved to be binding in practice due to the size of the Petroleum Fund.
- The analysis shows that substantial institutional bindings are possible.
- In Germany, there are tensions between strict budget discipline and the need to borrow money for new investments, particularly to ensure the transition to renewable energy.
- In Norway, there are tensions about which ethical considerations the fund includes in its investments, but the more fundamental tension is about the large oil and gas sector, on which the petroleum fund's income is based.
- In the contemporary world, where today's generations pass on a partially destroyed planet to their descendants, the arguments about preventing debt or securing savings for future generations should be discussed in the context of which resources are transferred to future generations.

References

Basic Law, German. (2022). Basic Law for the Federal Republic of Germany in the revised version published in the Federal Law Gazette Part III, classification number 100-1, as last amended by the Act of 19 December 2022 (Federal Law Gazette I p. 2478). Retrieved 16.11.2023 from https://www.gesetze-im-internet.de/englisch_gg/englisch_gg.html

Bolton, P., Samama, F., & Stiglitz, E. (2012). *Sovereign wealth funds and long-term investing*. Colombia University Press.

Bom, P. (2019). Fiscal rules and the intergenerational welfare effects of public investment. *Economic Modelling*, *81*, 455–470.

Breuer, C. (2021). Nützt die Schuldenbremse den kommenden Generationen? *Wirtschaftsdienst*, *101*(7), 490–491.

Bundestag, German. (2009). Entwurf eines ... Gesetzes zur Änderung des Grundgesetzes (Artikel 91c, 91d, 104b, 109, 109a, 115, 143d). Drucksache 16/12410. Retrieved 21.11.2023 from https://dserver.bundestag.de/btd/16/124/1612410.pdf

Bundestag, German. (2020). Beschluss des Bundestages gemäß Artikel 115 Absatz 2 Satz 6 und 7 des Grundgesetzes. Drucksache 19/20128. Retrieved 30.04.2024 from https://dserver.bundestag.de/btd/19/201/1920128.pdf

Bundestag, German. (2022a). Zweites Nachtragshaushaltgesetz 2021. Retrieved 30.04.2024 from https://www.bundestag.de/dokumente/textarchiv/2022/kw04-de-nachtragshaushaltsgesetz-877110

Bundestag, German. (2022b). Entwurf eines Gesetzes zur Änderung des Grundgesetzes (Artikel 87a). Drucksache 20/1410. Retrieved 30.04.2024 from https://dserver.bundestag.de/btd/20/014/2001410.pdf

Burret, H. T. (2013). Die deutsche Schuldenbremse als Allheilmittel – Eine Analyse im historischen Kontext. *Journal für Generationengerechtigkeit*, *13*(2), 48–65.

Burret, H. T., Feld, L. P., & Köhler, E. A. (2013). Sustainability of public debt in Germany – Historical considerations and time series evidence. *Jahrbücher f. Nationalökonomie u. Statistik*, *233*(3), 291–335.

Caney, S. (2018). Justice and future generations. *Annual Review of Political Science*, *21*, 475–493.

Constitutional Court, German Federal. (2023). Second Supplementary Budget Act 2021 is void. Press Release No. 101/2023 of 15 November 2023. Retrieved 15.11.2023 from https://www.bundesverfassungsgericht.de/SharedDocs/Pressemitteilungen/EN/2023/bvg23-101.html

Davoodi, H. R., Elger, P., Fotiou, A., Garcia-Macia, D., Han, X., Lagerborg, A., Lam, W. R., & Medas, P. A. (2022). Fiscal rules and fiscal councils: Recent trends and performance during the pandemic, *IMF Working Paper 22/11*. International Monetary Fund. Retrieved 06.05.2024 from https://www.imf.org/en/Publications/WP/Issues/2022/01/21/Fiscal-Rules-and-Fiscal-Councils-512128

European Commission. (2005). European economy. Directorate-General for Economic and Financial Affairs. Number 3. Retrieved 08.12.2023 from https://ec.europa.eu/economy_finance/publications/pages/publication421_en.pdf

European Commission. (2022). Report on public finances in EMU. *Institutional paper* 181. Retrieved 08.12.2023 from https://economy-finance.ec.europa.eu/system/files/2022-07/ip181_en_1.pdf

Feld, L. P., Reuter, W. H., & Yeter, M. (2020). Öffentliche Investitionen: Die Schuldenbremse ist nicht das Problem. *Perspektiven der Wirtschaftspolitik*, *20*(4), 292–303.

Finneron-Burns, E. (forthcoming). Global justice, sovereign wealth funds and saving for the future. *Critical Review of International Social and Political Philosophy*. https://doi.org/10.1080/13698230.2023.2226473

Fratzscher, M. (2023). Kluge Schulden heute sind der Wohlstand von morgen. Blog Marcel Fratzscher vom 21. Dezember 2023. Retrieved 20.04.2024 from https://www.diw.de/de/diw_01.c.889017.de/nachrichten/kluge_schulden_heute_sind_der_wohlstand_von_morgen.html

German Council of Economic Experts. (2019). *Sachverständigenrat* annual report 2019/20. Dealing with structural change. Retrieved 30.04.2024 from https://www.sachverstaendigenrat-wirtschaft.de/en/annualreport-2019.html

German Council of Economic Experts. (2023). *Sachverständigenrat* annual report 2023/2024. Retrieved 14.11.2023 from https://www.sachverstaendigenrat-wirtschaft.de/en/annualreport-2023-pressrelease.html

Gough, I. (2017). *Heat, greed and human need. Climate change, capitalism and sustainable wellbeing*. Edward Elgar.

Graeber, D. (2011). *Debt: The first 5,000 years*. Melvillehouse.

Graver, H. P. (2004). Etiske retningslinjer for oljefondet. *Kritisk Juss*, *30*(3), 264–276.

Grohmann, L. (2013). Generationsgerechte Finanzpolitik im Bundesstaat – ohne Aussicht auf Erfolg? Zur Effektivität der sogenannten «Schuldenbremse» in den Bundesländern. *Journal für Generationsgerechtigkeit*, *13*(2), 65–79.

Habib, A. (2013). Sharing the earth: Sustainability and the currency of inter-generational environmental justice. *Environmental Values*, *22*(6), 751–764.

IMF. (2022). International Monetary Fund. Fiscal affairs department. Retrieved 01.12.2023 from https://www.imf.org/external/datamapper/fiscalrules/map/map.htm

Innst. S. 195. (2004–2005). Innstilling fra finanskomiteen om pensjonsreform - trygghet for pensjonene. Recommendation from the Standing Committee in the Storting on finance and economic affairs on pension reform - security for pensions. Retrieved 06.05.2024 from https://www.stortinget.no/no/Saker-og-publikasjoner/Publikasjoner/Innstillinger/Stortinget/2004-2005/inns-200405-195/?lvl=0

IPBES. (2022). *Summary for policymakers of the methodological assessment report on the diverse values and valuation of nature of the intergovernmental science-policy platform on biodiversity and ecosystem services*. U. Pascual, P. Balvanera, M. Christie, B. Baptiste, D. González-Jiménez, C. B. Anderson, S. Athayde, D. N. Barton, R. Chaplin-Kramer, S. Jacobs, E. Kelemen, R. Kumar, E. Lazos, A. Martin, T. H. Mwampamba, B. Nakangu, P. O'Farrell, C. M. Raymond, S. M. Subramanian, ... A. Vatn. (Eds.). IPBES secretariat. Retrieved 29.11.2023 from https://doi.org/10.5281/zenodo.6522392

Jamasb, T., & Sen, A. (2022). The new energy state: A review of offshore governance regimes for renewables as natural resources. Copenhagen Business School. *CSEI Working Paper* 2022-02. Department of Economics. Copenhagen Business School.

Lansley, S. (2016). *A sharing economy. How social wealth funds can tackle inequality and balance the books*. Policy Press.

Lie, E. (2012). *Norsk økonomisk politikk etter 1905*. Universitetsforlaget.

Lie, E. (2015). *Handlingsreglers politiske og historiske betydning* (pp. 232–236). Attachment 1 to NOU (2015: 9).

Lie, E., Kobberrød, J. T., Thomassen, E., & Rongved, G. F. (2016). *Norges bank 1816–2016*. Fagbokforlaget.

Meld. St. 1. (2023–2024). The National Budget 2024. Report to the Storting (white paper). Retrieved 06.05.2024 from https://www.regjeringen.no/en/dokumenter/meld.-st.-1-20232024/id2998356/

Meld. St. 26. (2016–2017). The management of the government pension fund in 2016. Report to the Storting (white paper). Retrieved 06.05.2024 from https://www.regjeringen.no/en/dokumenter/meld.-st.-26-20162017/id2545354/

Ministry of Finance, German Federal. (2022). Germany's federal debt rule (debt brake). Retrieved 30.04.2024 from https://www.bundesfinanzministerium.de/Content/EN/Downloads/Public-Finances/germanys-federal-debt-rule.pdf?__blob=publicationFile&v=5

NBIM. (2017). Norges Bank recommends the removal of oil stocks from the benchmark index of the Government Pension Fund Global (GPFG). Retrieved 30.04.2024 from https://www.nbim.no/en/the-fund/news-list/2017/norges-bank-recommends-the-removal-of-oil-stocks-from-the-benchmark-index-of-the-government-pension-fund-global-gpfg/

NBIM. (2024a). Norges Bank Investment Management. About the fund. Retrieved 22.03.2024 from https://www.nbim.no/en/the-fund/Market-Value/

NBIM. (2024b). Norges Banks Investment Management. About us. Retrieved 16.04.2024 from https://www.nbim.no/en/organisation/about-us/

Norwegian Council on Ethics for GPFG. (2023). Council on Ethics for the Government Pension Fund Global. Retrieved 27.11.2023 from https://etikkradet.no/en/

Norwegian Petroleum (2023). Web page Norwegian Petroleum, the Government's revenues. Retrieved 08.08.2023 from https://www.norskpetroleum.no/en/economy/governments-revenues/

Norwegian Petroleum. (2024). Exports of oil and gas. Retrieved 16.04.2024 from https://www.norskpetroleum.no/en/production-and-exports/exports-of-oil-and-gas/

NOU. (2017: 13). New central bank act. Norwegian public report. Retrieved 06.05.2024 from https://www.regjeringen.no/en/dokumenter/nou-2017-13/id2558711/

O'Neill, J. F. (2017). Pluralism and incommensurability. In C. L. Spash (Ed.), *Routledge handbook of ecological economics: nature and society* (pp. 227–236). Routledge.

Ot. Prp. 2. (2005–2006). The Government Pension Fund Act (2006). Parliamentary report. Retrieved 06.05.2024 from https://www.regjeringen.no/no/dokumenter/otprp-nr-2-2005-2006-/id132497/

Ot. Prp. 29. (1989–1990). The Government Petroleum Fund Act (1990). Parliamentary report. Retrieved 06.05.2024 from https://www.stortinget.no/no/Saker-og-publikasjoner/Stortingsforhandlinger/Lesevisning/?p=1989-90&paid=4&wid=a&psid=DIVL470

Øvald, C. B., Tranøy, B. S., & Raknes, K. (2019). The Norwegian Petroleum Fund as institutionalized self-restraint. In I. Compton, E. Mallory, & P. T. Hart (Eds.), *Great policy successes* (pp. 244–263). Oxford University Press.

Pascual, U., Balvanera, P., Anderson, C. B., Chaplin-Kramer, R., Christie, M., González-Jiménez, D., Martin, A., Raymond, C. M., Termansen, M., Vatn, A., Athayde, S., Baptiste, B., Barton, D. N., Jacobs, S., Kelemen, E., Kumar, R., Lazos, E., Mwampamba, T. H., Nakangu, B., … Zent, E. (2023). Diverse values of nature for sustainability. *Nature*, 620, pp. 813–823.

Rawls, J. (1971). *A theory of justice*. Harvard University Press.

Rawls, J. (2001). *Justice as fairness. A restatement*. Harvard University Press.

Schiefloe, P. M. (2016). Norge og oljen. In I. Fønes, & L. Kjølsrød (Eds.), *Det norske samfunn* (pp. 139–190). Gyldendal Akademisk.

Sigl-Glöckner, P., Krahé, M., Schneemelcher, P., Schuster, F., Hilbert, V., & Meyer, H. (2021). *A new fiscal policy for Germany. Dezernat Zukunft*. Institute for Macrofinance.

Sovereign Wealth Fund Institute. (2023a). Ranking. Retrieved 08.08.2023 from https://www.swfinstitute.org/fund-rankings/sovereign-wealth-fund

Sovereign Wealth Fund Institute. (2023b). What is a sovereign wealth fund? Current trends. Retrieved 08.08.2023 from https://www.swfinstitute.org/research/sovereign-wealth-fund

Spash, C. L. (2002). Economics, ethics and future generations. In C. L. Spash (Ed.), *Greenhouse economics: Value and ethics* (pp. 221–250). Routledge.

St. Meld. 2. (2003–2004). Revised national budget 2004 (white paper). Retrieved 06.05.2024 from https://www.regjeringen.no/no/dokumenter/stmeld-nr-2-2003-2004-/id403291/

St. Meld. 25. (1973–1974). Petroleum industry in Norwegian society (white paper). Retrieved 06.05.2024 from https://www.regjeringen.no/no/dokumenter/meld-st-25-1973-1974/id708378/

St. Meld. 29. (2000–2001). Guidelines for the economic policy (white paper). Retrieved 06.05.2024 from https://www.regjeringen.no/no/dokumenter/stmeld-nr-29-2000-2001-/id194346/

St. Meld. 32. (1984–1985). On the future of petroleum activities (white paper). Retrieved 06.05.2024 from https://www.stortinget.no/nn/Saker-og-publikasjonar/Stortingsforhandlingar/Lesevisning/?p=1984-85&paid=3&wid=b&psid=DIVL1174&pgid=b_0775&s=True

Tremmel, J. (2009). *A theory of intergenerational justice*. Earthscan.

Vallee, S., Cohen-Setton, J., & Buhl, D. (2021). Germany's debt brake and Europe's fiscal stance after COVID-19. *German Council of Foreign Relations Policy Brief*, 1. https://dgap.org/sites/default/files/article_pdfs/dgap-policy%20brief-2021-01-en.pdf

Wilson, D. S., & Hessen, D. O. (2014). Blueprint for the global village. *Cliodynamics: The Journal of Quantitative History and Cultural Evolution*, *5*(1), 123–157.

9
CONCLUSION

Introduction

This book is written against the backdrop that current generations can influence the welfare of future people more than any previous generation. This gives today's generations a responsibility, which is increased by the fact that future generations do not have the opportunity to influence current politics. This knowledge is widespread, and it has led to a multitude of commitments to include future generations in political, legal, and economic measures both globally and nationally. However, these normative commitments are scarcely reflected in practical politics.

Four policy areas are analysed with explicitly formulated normative commitments to take concerns about future generations into account in current political decisions and examined whether and how they are combined with politically and legally binding actions. The UN 2030 Agenda is at the global level. The remaining three are at the national level concerning political institutions, protection clauses in institutions, and financial constraints. Germany and Norway have been selected as examples of countries that have committed their states to take future generations' concerns into account and, to various degrees, introduced self-imposed institutional constraints.

Two overarching questions are analysed. Firstly, when and how the commitments to future generations are followed up in practice, and what characterises situations where they are not followed up? Secondly, to what extent and how are there differences between the two countries and the four policy areas, and what can we learn from comparing them?

The scholarly debate about if and how today's generations have a responsibility towards those who come after us has been dominated by discussions

DOI: 10.4324/9781003400806-11
This chapter has been made available under a CC-BY-NC-ND 4.0 license.

of intergenerational justice. However, these studies suggest abstract principles do not capture the social and contextual aspects of how future generations might be included in today's decisions. The few studies that have discussed what intergenerational solidarity might imply are theoretical and philosophical, and challenging to apply to empirical studies. With this book, I attempt to contribute to these debates by suggesting a concept of solidarity that is more useful to analyse what is practically possible.

Central political notions such as nation and state sovereignty are challenged when the concept of solidarity is extended to include future generations. Modern political communities are built on a concept of time that grounds today's community with events in the past. This has created the dominant political frames of our time. When future generations are considered as a central political premise, this changes our relationship to time and means that our established political frames must be held up for critical assessment. Measures that consider future generations do not just break the boundaries of time, they also break national boundaries and show the necessity of establishing cosmopolitan political structures, which we have seen is challenging.

Two-dimensional solidarity concept

I have developed a political and normative concept of solidarity with future generations consisting of two dimensions. The first dimension comprises ideas of indirect reciprocity with future generations. This means giving something to a person, but it is not necessarily the same person who gives something in return. The second dimension concerns the willingness to establish self-imposed institutional bindings to ensure that governments endorse and sustain measures to safeguard future oriented goals for the sake of future generations. The core of the concept is that both dimensions must be fulfilled to show social solidarity with future generations.

Combinations of commitments to future generations based on indirect reciprocity and the establishment of institutional bindings vary in different policy areas and between the countries. These combinations are analysed by studying, firstly, what the commitments to future generations involve in each policy area and country, and secondly, by analysing how the commitments are followed up by binding institutional constraints. The empirical studies show that various societal concerns are in tension with the institutional constraints in the different policy areas and countries.

Substantial financial constraints

The financial constraints are more comprehensive and binding in practice than the political and legal bindings in the other policy areas. Germany and

Norway are examples of how several countries have recently introduced fiscal rules for financial reasons. While the German goal is to prevent financial debt, the Norwegian aim is to ensure financial savings. Both countries justify this by referring to future generations. This can be interpreted as ideas of indirect reciprocity.

The strength of the constraints is different in the two countries. The German debt brake can only be changed through a constitutional reform, but it can be circumvented when political crises occur such as COVID-19 and Russia's invasion of Ukraine. Such exceptions show how contemporary crises create obstacles for a long-term policy. The Norwegian budget restrictions can be changed by a simple majority decision in the *Storting*. Although the restrictions are designed as guidelines with weak formal bindings, they have proved binding in practice. The background is the fund's market value, which has increased significantly over the past 20 years.

The target for the German debt brake is precisely measured in the debt-to-GDP ratio every year. In Norway, the fiscal guideline is a precise target measured as a percentage of the fund size. The precise measurement strengthens the financial constraints but reveals the one-dimensional character of the restrictions.

In both countries, the fiscal rules are in tension with other societal concerns. In Germany, there are tensions between strict budget discipline and the need to borrow money for new investments. Seen from the perspective of preventing ecological damage for future generations, it might be better for future people if the current focus on stabilising the debt-to-GDP ratio was replaced by solving the country's main challenge, which is to ensure the transition to renewable energy. The tension in Norway concerns the large oil and gas sector, on which the petroleum fund's income is based. From the perspective of the government and the *Storting*, oil and gas as natural capital are converted into financial capital. Seen from the perspective of preventing ecological damage for future generations, future Norwegian generations might prefer oil and gas under the seabed rather than financial investments.

While financial constraints are the most substantial form of institutional bindings, they represent a one-dimensional transfer of values between generations. By justifying these constraints by referring to a concern for future generations, I would argue that these concerns should include caring for nature. We therefore need a broader understanding of how to spend or preserve different types of resources in solidarity with future generations.

Financial restrictions show that it is possible to introduce and practise substantial institutional constraints if there is political will. As we have seen, it is necessary to strengthen the institutional ties in the different policy areas to show solidarity with future generations. It may be possible to learn from how fiscal restrictions are practised to find examples from practice. However, fiscal restrictions are problematic as a role model. Fiscal restrictions are justified based on both economic considerations and a concern for future generations. As long as states justify the restrictions based on consideration of future generations, we need a broader approach to spending or preserving various types of resources in solidarity with future generations.

From the public sphere to the courtroom

The most significant changes are in the legal area. The German and Norwegian cases are examples of a global trend of children and youths trying to change climate and environmental policy through legal systems. Even though several lawsuits have been dismissed, the move from the public sphere to legal mobilisations through the courts provides a political space where future generations are seen and heard. Both countries have facilitated these legal means by including protection clauses for future generations in their constitutions.

The two climate lawsuits analysed in this book show how the claimants in both countries appealed to intergenerational solidarity based on an equal distribution of efforts to prevent climate and environmental destruction. I interpret the claimants' ideas in terms of indirect reciprocity, which is not only limited to national solidarity but also includes aspects of cosmopolitan solidarity.

We have seen that the governments of both countries reject the legal complaints by pointing out this is a matter for political institutions. The decisions from the countries' highest courts reveal more complex arguments. The German Federal Constitutional Court's rulings entailed far stronger restrictions on German politics than the Norwegian Supreme Court's judgment on Norwegian politics.

The German Constitutional Court judgement was that the legislators had to change the Federal Climate Change Act. In response, federal policymakers passed a law that immediately steps up the goals of the current reduction in greenhouse gases. This shows that the protection clause has introduced considerable institutional bindings. In contrast, the Supreme Court of Norway called the protection clause a "safety valve." The court did not apply the safety valve in this lawsuit, which means the protection clause in the Norwegian constitution has weak institutional bindings.

There was far more at stake in the Norwegian climate lawsuit than in the German one. The tensions in the Norwegian lawsuit concerned central parts of Norwegian petroleum policy, the country's most important source of income. The tensions in the German climate lawsuit involved questions about distribution of effort to reduce greenhouse gas emissions between generations and had minor consequences for German politics.

I find it noteworthy how the claimants in the lawsuits in both countries introduced alternative frames for problem definition and moral evaluations. The German Constitutional Court supported these frames when it described how individuals' fundamental rights to freedom in the future lie in the present and emphasised that this must have consequences for current policies. In Norway, we can see a weak and vulnerable development of new frames in the courts. This is shown in how the Oslo District Court in 2024 interpreted the Supreme Court's 2020 assessments in a new lawsuit. In support of the claimants from the environmental organisations, the District Court concluded that before approving oil and gas fields, the state must assess the impact of greenhouse gas emissions including the combustion abroad of Norwegian-produced oil and gas. The state has appealed the ruling.

With these lawsuits some children and youths have moved their activities from protests and demonstrations in the public sphere to the use of protection clauses to promote new problem definitions and moral evaluations in the courtroom. They have thereby contributed to a slow shift in the framing of if and how the state is responsible for social solidarity with future generations.

In the Norwegian climate lawsuit, the environmental organisations argued that Norway has a global responsibility that must be assessed because the country is a significant oil and gas exporter. This contradicts the current international order where each state is responsible for its national emissions. The complainants lost the case.

The German ruling shows that the Federal Constitutional Court had a more complex argument. The court stated that dependence on the international community makes it necessary for a state to carry out its national climate measures. Although no state can resolve the problems of climate change on its own, the court argued, this does not invalidate the national obligation to take climate action. The decision made by the German court is binding on German policy. It shows how international agreements have national consequences and include aspects of cosmopolitan solidarity.

As the analysis of the climate lawsuits shows, national protection clauses for future generations in national constitutions can be appealed to the European Court of Human Rights(ECtHR). As a supranational body, the conclusions from the ECtHR are binding on the nation states. This is the case in the four cases ECtHR has deemed a priority for hearing. In one of the cases, *KlimaSeniorinnen v. Switzerland*, the Court concluded that the Swiss Confederation had failed to comply with its duties under the Convention concerning climate change. This will have consequences for how the ECtHR judges in future climate lawsuits, such as the Norwegian case which is still pending as of April 2024.

Weak political institutions

By establishing political institutions for future generations, states have committed themselves to implementing long-term policies important for future generations. These commitments are interpreted as a form of indirect reciprocity. The institutions have the potential to ensure proxy representation for future generations. Still, they have a weak influence in practice.

Neither Germany nor Norway has institutions with a special mandate to represent future generations. I have examined both countries' measures to implement the Sustainable Development Goals (SDGs) and analysed to what extent and how these can be seen as ways to ensure a long-term policy that can impact future people.

Germany has a triangle of institutions provided with the tasks to ensure the implementation of the SDGs in parliament, in government, and one as an independent state institution. The country has also established two institutions that are particularly relevant for climate and environmental issues. In general, they have weak influence on whether the long-term policy becomes binding in practice. As an example, the German Parliamentary Advisory Council on Sustainable Development operates according to a consensus principle. The Council's role is to call attention to future consequences of current decisions. This might strengthen the commitments to the future, but this is not enough to secure institutional constraints that bind political decisions to long-term goals.

In Norway, the Ombudsperson for Children is often mentioned in reviews of countries with institutions for future generations, but it does not function as such. Norway lacks institutions to ensure the implementation of the SDGs. The implementation of the SDGs is assigned to the Ministry of Local Government and Modernisation. This means that the main efforts are made at the local level, while the tensions involved in implementing the environmental SDGs are national and cannot be solved locally. The implementation is less transparent than in Germany.

In Germany and Norway, there are tensions between long-term environmental considerations and the production and use of energy from fossil fuels. The weakness of institutions for future generations can be linked to these political tensions. The weaknesses of these institutions are examples of a larger pattern. Institutions that have the task of ensuring that consideration is given to future generations play a role as reminders. They can be important because they remind political actors and the public in general of the importance of considering future generations. Awareness raising is essential to show solidarity with future generations, but it is unclear and for the time being doubtful that these institutions will have a decisive influence on how current generations act. The weakness of these institutions shows a gap between commitments to future generations and their implementation in practice. The institutions must be strengthened to show solidarity with future generations.

Global commitments and national restraints

The global consensus in the UN 2030 Agenda is an essential driving force for increasing global commitments for future generations. The extremely ambitious programme of the 2030 Agenda is the culmination of a long process from 1972 to 2015. The agenda was presented as a charter to change the world in the twenty-first century, but such a programme is challenging to implement in the nation states.

Nevertheless, these commitments have some influence on national political implementation by the way they represent a common frame to categorise and describe the world's challenges and solutions. The way bodies within the UN system monitor the countries' achievement of the SDGs and publish them in open global databases create institutional constraints on the UN member states. The combination of the common frames and the monitoring of the member states' achievements make the commitments morally binding. However, these bindings are weak, and all SDGs are seriously off track. The most essential form of sanction is shame, which has proven to be a meagre means of power in international politics.

The 2030 Agenda is an example of the ambiguous relationship between national and cosmopolitan solidarity with future generations. The discrepancy between the global commitments to future generations in the 2030 Agenda and the nation states' restraints from implementation in practice stems from the tensions between the nation states' sovereignty and global commitments to future generations. Nation states do not follow through on implementing what they have agreed on globally, and no global institution has the authority to put pressure on countries to implement the 2030 Agenda with the SDGs.

The transition from international agreements to nation states is the critical point. The challenges arise when cosmopolitan ideas of intergenerational indirect reciprocity are to be implemented in practice at the national level. National political institutions for future generations reflect this challenge. Institutional arrangements to ensure the implementation of sustainable development goals are based on a cosmopolitan framing, but they have weak institutional constraints on national policy.

There is thus a call from the UN system for future-focused global institutions that can incorporate the concern for future generations. This has culminated in recent years, and the proposals have been presented as the step from commitment to reality, which implies a call for action. However, I would not interpret this as a call for cosmopolitan solidarity with future generations. None of these proposals from the UN Secretary-General involves a transfer of sovereignty to a global organisation. This means that the tensions between the sovereignty of nation states and global obligations towards future generations are maintained. As various agreements are made piecemeal globally and are expected to be implemented in the nation states, it becomes challenging to implement global institutional bindings in practice.

Showing social solidarity with future generations

This book shows differences in how commitments to future generations are followed up in practice between countries and among policy areas. The differences between the countries can be understood from the countries' political and economic context. In this book, these differences are analysed within the framework of the German dilemma and the Norwegian paradox.

The institutional bindings are weak in all policy areas, but this book reveals variations among them. The financial restrictions represent the most substantial institutional constraints. They are one-dimensional and require a discussion about which resources should be passed on to future generations.

The legal area shows the most significant changes. The legal mobilisations through the courts provide a political space where new frames for moral evaluations and problem-solving are presented. This has had varying degrees of success in practice, and it remains uncertain what the consequences will be in the long term.

The political institutions are generally weak. They function as reminders for political actors and the public of the importance of considering future generations. To gain substantial political influence, they must be strengthened.

The 2030 Agenda is an essential driving force for increasing global commitments for future generations. There is a gap between global commitments to future generations and national implementation in practice, and there are few indications that this gap will be closed.

To analyse the political processes between commitments and implementation in practice, we need a fine-grained theoretical analytical tool. The concept of solidarity with future generations developed and applied in this book has proved to be useful to reveal the variations. By applying this concept to empirical studies, we can conclude that it is possible to establish self-imposed institutional constraints with the aim to ensure that future generations have access to basic resources and the opportunity to shape their own lives. The complexity of the policy areas means it is valuable to show where the weaknesses and strengths can be found. Institutional bindings must be strengthened to show social solidarity with future generations.

INDEX